Special Educational Needs in the Twentieth Century

Also available in the Institute of Education series:

Education for the Nation Richard Aldrich
Transforming Learning Susan Askew and Eileen Carnell
The End of Knowledge in Higher Education Ronald Barnett and Anne Griffin
Education and the End of Work John White

SPECIAL EDUCATIONAL NEEDS IN THE TWENTIETH CENTURY

A Cultural Analysis

Jenny Corbett

CASSELL

Cassell

Wellington House
125 Strand
London WC2R 0BB

PO Box 605
Herndon
VA 20172

First published 1998

British Library Cataloguing-in-Publication Data
A catalogue record for this book is available from the British Library.

ISBN 0–304–70080–0 (hardback)
0–304–70081–9 (paperback)

Typeset by York House Typographic Ltd, London.
Printed and bound in Great Britain by
Redwood Books, Trowbridge, Wilts

Contents

ONE   Special Educational Needs in the Twentieth Century: 1
      A Cultural Analysis

TWO   Teaching 'Backward' Children to Read: 7
      A Struggle to Raise Standards

THREE   Addressing Challenging Behaviours: 16
        Moral Values and Public Panic

FOUR   A Century of Change: 25
       Treatments and Tensions

FIVE   Values, Choice and Entitlement   35

SIX   Community and the Culture of Caring   46

SEVEN   Empowerment and Colonialism: 58
        Letting Go

EIGHT   Care with Vision: 67
        A New Role for Professionals

        Bibliography   79
        Index   85

This book is dedicated to the memory of Christopher Davidson-Paine, who died of AIDS on 5 August 1996, aged only 38. He was a teacher who demonstrated care and vision and he is greatly missed.

All the apparatus they need is raised books, raised maps and a tablet to write on. These can be furnished as well at a regular school as at an institution. The reason for the institutions lies in the history of education, not in the essential needs of the blind.

(Helen Keller (1913) *Out of the Dark*, pp. 202–3)

Those of us who see ourselves as part of a 'movement', understanding the commonality of our experience and trying to work in solidarity to effect change, nevertheless are also aware of the enormous differences in our experiences as disabled people, particularly where they cross those other cultural borders of race, gender and sexuality.

(Ann Pointon and Chris Davies (1997) *Framed: Interrogating Disability in the Media*, p. 3)

ONE

Special Educational Needs in the Twentieth Century: A Cultural Analysis

My intention in this book is to open out the context in which special educational needs are discussed. A specialist area in education, special needs has always been at risk from marginalization, isolation and a narrow focus upon programmes, practice and assessment measures. The 1994 Code of Practice in Britain has heightened a concentration on detail and an intensity of focus. In our eagerness to examine the specific, we run the risk of missing the whole: we cannot see the wood for the trees.

I want to set special educational needs into a wider context in three key areas:

- *historically*, to look back over the last century in order that the present and potential future can be better understood;
- *internationally*, so that other cultures can be explored and their ways of responding to disability understood;
- *at a community level*, by placing the experience of schooling into a deeper community context which includes issues of equity and entitlement, social roles and the valuing of individual and collective differences.

These are three complex and interrelated aspects of the context in which special educational needs can be understood and evaluated. They are each, of themselves, worthy of deeper and more lengthy analysis than I can apply here. My aims for the book are both ambitious and modest: ambitious, in opening up a much wider context than is usually approached in this area which raises many contentious issues; modest, in recognizing from the outset that this text can be no more than an introductory exploration of a broad base which may then offer stimulus for further, more extensive study in the future.

My wish is to encourage those who teach courses on special education in universities, who train teachers to become special needs co-ordinators in schools and colleges, and who currently work with learners who are labelled as having special needs, to consider the following issues:

- that what is seen as a crisis in education in one period of history often re-emerges in

another guise as a crisis in education at a later period, accompanied by a popular nostalgia for the mythical *golden age* of educational standards;
■ that labels are culturally specific and can say as much about their society, its values, attitudes and context, as they do about the recipients of the label;
■ that how we treat the most vulnerable members of our society defines the extent to which we can call ourselves a civilized culture.

A Historical, Cultural and Social Context

Learning from history is a theme which runs through the book. Beginning with one of the currently critical issues of British politics, that of improving school standards, Chapter 2 examines the attitudes to the teaching of literacy prevalent in British schools of the early 1900s. It notes that compulsory schooling was not universally accepted and was seen by some as a highly suspect form of social engineering. The poor were better kept ignorant for it prevented them getting too restless. There were unskilled jobs in abundance at that period of industrialization and such workers did not need to read. Now, with the demise of an industrial society, they are being given education without employment or, perhaps, as an alternative to employment. The British public are always being told that educational standards used to be better in the earlier days of this century, yet the drop-out rate in early Board Schools contradicts this rose-tinted view. It may be the model grammar schools that the government holds up as bastions of standards, yet the wastage within the rest of the system was considerable. Maybe it is because league tables and competition between schools are now fostering a cruel hierarchy in the state sector that 'standards' have become a rallying cry for politicians. The 'sink' city schools, at the bottom of the league and drained of potential pupils by stronger and more attractive competitors, may now resemble those early Board Schools of the late 1800s and early 1900s. Like them, they cater for predominantly poor, working-class children, whose parents have no choice but to use their local schools, whose job prospects are strictly limited and academic achievements well below those of more favourable schools. As schools are encouraged to detach themselves from the state sector, the least marketable schools are finding themselves with higher proportions of children labelled as 'SEN' (special educational needs). Like the Board Schools of the early 1900s, which struggled to contain what they called 'street ruffians', these schools often struggle to cope with a disproportionate number of children who require additional help with literacy and numeracy, and are themselves labelled as 'failing schools' by the current inspection regime.

In Chapter 3, the issue of disruptive or challenging behaviour in schools is discussed in relation to historical debates on behaviour and discipline. This links in to the debates in Chapter 2 which explore the impact of compulsory schooling and the difficulties inherent in containing in schools children who would not previously have been educated. This chapter introduces a comparison with parts of Africa and the lives of some adolescents there who are accepted as 'street children'. Their adult roles are contrasted with the prolonged childhoods of young people in the Western world. This opens up the issue of value judgements and asks how we impose our own cultural values on another very different culture. Whose values should dominate and must values always be context-specific? The tensions within value systems are a theme which runs through the book and I see addressing these tensions as absolutely central to our understanding of special educational needs. How a society treats its most vulnerable members defines the nature of that society. Where the whole society is highly vulnerable (e.g. during a period of famine or civil war) people with additional needs are having to share limited resources with others who also see themselves in need. The context will determine the response. One of the main findings of my research, which again threads through the book, is that simple societies can often respond with more humanity to their most vulnerable members than highly complex, technological societies. Perhaps they are composed of more people who can offer *time*, that most valuable commodity in short supply in advanced cultures.

Chapter 4 explores advances in medical treatments for disabled children and looks at why medicine and a medical approach to disability became so powerfully established early in this century. Using the example of tuberculosis as a case study, medical advances are presented as socially transforming, influencing the cultural context in which children with this disease were educated, treated and supported to improved health. This disease of the early 1900s has become a cause for concern again at the end of the century in the poorest parts of the world and in poor areas of cities like London and New York. AIDS and its impact on children is also explored as an aspect of medical intervention related to poverty and global inequalities. The social context of medical issues is one which challenges notions that the medical model of disability is only about within-child deficits and does not address the social, political and economic factors which foster disease and disability. Tensions between the social model of disability, which sees social barriers as the key issue, and the medical model, which is disease- or disability-focused, are examined and assessed in relation to current developments. Taking examples from Asia and Africa, I explore the complex situation whereby one half of the world urgently needs more medical intervention to confront disease and disability while the other half is more concerned with promoting a social model within a disability-rights political agenda for equal status, independence from charities and more choice in daily living arrangements. These two aspects are not incompatible but perhaps indicate different stages of development towards a disability-rights consciousness. People may be reluctant to campaign for independence from professional intervention before they obtain the basic levels of treatment which can alleviate pain, discomfort and deteriorating physical health. The value of comparing situations in different countries is that it presents us with a realization that priorities are culturally and contextually defined and that people may become politicized only when they are receptive and not before.

Chapter 5 focuses directly upon the concept of values and how this relates to choice and entitlement. It begins by examining the value judgements of a renowned doctor at the end of the last century whose perceptions and naming of syndromes were influenced by the freak shows of the period. The influence of popular culture on our sensibilities is a theme which again threads through the book as it seems to me to be an important aspect often overlooked in debates on education in general and special education in particular. Theorists and practitioners are a part of their own popular culture, influenced by gut feelings, sentiments and personal taste as well as by rational thinking and analysis.

The concept of 'E-mapping' is introduced in Chapter 5, and this then runs through the remainder of the book. It is an idea related to our current concern for individual entitlement in special educational needs, which is often interpreted to mean a struggle to gain as many resources as possible for one child from a restricted pool available to all comers. It is a feature of the market culture, characteristic of British education in the late 1990s, and special educational needs is just one part of this. 'E-mapping' is about status related to entitlement. Even when there are sufficient resources to go round, some are seen as more socially worthy than others and they, therefore, get their entitlement whilst others are seen as undeserving or inadequate or may simply be unaware of how the system operates.

This issue is explored through the example of specific learning difficulties (dyslexia) and tribunals in the British education system, whereby parents can take a local education authority to court to seek increased resources, or alternative resources to those they have been offered. The concept of entitlement is then set within an international context to illustrate that labelling and provision for special educational needs varies considerably in different areas of the world. In countries with high levels of poverty, civil war and limited medical care, blanket labels of disability are often used. In countries like North America and Britain new labels seem to proliferate and some are seen as far more desirable and marketable than others.

Taking two controversial labels of the mid to late twentieth century, autism and attention deficit hyperactivity disorder (ADHD), I explore the ways in which the special-needs labels of a culture can reflect its individualistic or communal value systems. As a generalization, individualistic values are a feature of Western culture and the Northern hemisphere whilst communal values are more commonly found in the Southern hemisphere.

Chapter 6 examines the various locations of community values. In this chapter I have chosen to select what is generally seen as a profoundly individualistic cultural context in which to explore issues of community and a culture of caring. North America is a long-established capitalist culture where the cult of individual self-interest is deeply embedded in the national consciousness. It is, therefore, a challenge to use the USA as a basis for exploring examples of community values and a caring cultural context. However, it is important to illustrate that within a country which would appear to offer restricted opportunities for communal values, these are readily to be found. The focus is upon community at several levels: in the local, regional context; within institutions of schools, colleges and universities; inside classrooms; in the disability movement, as a subculture with its own distinct and disparate community.

This chapter explores the nature of caring communities and what features they need to have in order to care for their more vulnerable members without drawing upon professional support. The role of the professional carer and expert becomes a central facet of debate throughout the remainder of the book. Caring communities are demonstrated to be those which do not delegate care to professionals. The professional gaze is often so judgemental that it can damage rather than support the recipients of care, particularly if they have learning disabilities and are unfamiliar with assertiveness strategies and unable to protect their own interests. However, professionals are often highly critical of their own community and eager to be more responsive and adaptable. Examples are explored of teachers who foster a responsive and empowering approach. The area of disability culture is well established in North America and reflects many issues of both community cohesion and tensions. The chapter concludes with a range of international comparisons to set alongside the examples drawn from North America. They include developments and research findings from Britain, France, the Netherlands, China, Hungary and the Middle East. Beginning with educational communities and their relationship with their social context, I explore parental values in different countries, the opportunities for disabled people to integrate into their local communities and the complex relationship between achievement and self-esteem. Within this debate, the value of simple communities is seen to be considerable in supporting the self-worth and social role of more vulnerable members.

Chapter 7 links the notion of social worth and community values with empowerment and what this means in terms of unequal power relationships. It explores the loss of colonial power and the pain of letting go of authority and control, whether this relates to men ruling women, whites ruling blacks, non-disabled ruling disabled or parents ruling children. Using the model of the struggle for the emancipation of women in the early years of this century, the struggle of disabled people to control their own lives is presented as a fight for equal rights like many other similar fights in the past.

The academic area of disability studies is discussed, as it relates to the emancipation of disabled people. This is a contentious issue, in which there are many vested interests. It is recognized that academic debates, although influential in their field, tend to reach only a small audience. Popular culture, in the form of soap operas on television and best-selling novels, is presented as a rich opportunity to change negative stereotypes or to shock the general populace into confronting powerful images of angry and assertive disabled people. The chapter concludes with reflections on the pain of relinquishing power and the ways in which this process can be eased.

Chapter 8, which is the concluding chapter, provides three detailed case studies of professionals working with disabled people in ways which combine care with vision. They all reflect certain aspects of community collaboration, drawing the themes of the book back to the central issues outlined at the opening of this introductory chapter. Each individual has developed innovative ways of working which enhance empowerment and improve communication and collaboration to add richness to overall quality of life.

The three case studies are analysed in relation to the central themes which thread through the whole book. These are: the significance of E-mapping, or entitlement to services; the legacy of routine and ritual in professional service-delivery; the value of simplicity in community living; the importance of perceiving schools, colleges and universities as just part of community provision to be linked with other systems to form a coherent whole; the need to listen to visionary thinkers whose ideas may signal future growth areas.

This is a broad-based book, introducing many complex ideas which it has neither the scope nor the intention to pursue to any great detail. I do hope this will not frustrate the reader. I mean it to stimulate debate, to encourage further exploration and to invite critical comment. Special educational needs are not just about what happens in schools and classrooms, about procedures, practices and assessments. They are about our cultures, the societies we create and the relationships we form between people, countries, systems, hierarchies and global economies: about our ways of *being* in the world.

TWO

Teaching 'Backward' Children to Read: A Struggle to Raise Standards

To gain a true cultural understanding of the importance given to reading as an educative tool, it is necessary to return to that period when compulsory education was still a relatively new concept. Illiteracy was not regarded as a sign of learning disability; rather, it denoted social status and potential employment patterns. The capacity to read with understanding is a complex skill, combining, as Burt (1922) recognized, a range of complementary elements. Taking the classic example of spelling 'CAT', he illustrated this complexity with the following explanation of how a child fails as a reader:

> He fails not so much in power to associate as in power to integrate; not so much in the capacity to hook, as it were, 'C' mechanically on to 'A' and 'A' mechanically on to 'T', as in the capacity to synthesise in order the letter sounds, 'C-A-T', both with each other and with the letter forms, and the two groups in turn with word-form and word-sound as a whole, and each and all with meaning — with mental picture or generic idea — until the whole arrangement can operate as a compound unit of implicitly apprehended parts. (p. 285)

As a key British educational psychologist of his generation, Burt was to have a profound effect on how 'backwardness' was assessed by using the then relatively new tests of mental age (IQ) and educational ability. This was to lead the way for the whole remedial pathway which was to expand during the post-Second World War period. If a cultural dimension to learning to read is to be considered, it needs to begin by exploring the relationship between poverty and literacy. For reading to have meaning it has to be comprehensible and this cannot be merely assumed but has to be tested. Different reading schemes are successful and appropriate when they are located in a cultural context to which they are suited. Standards of literacy are often used politically to define national levels of educational attainment. In order to make any sense out of current alarms about 'falling standards' it is important to engage in a historical analysis to compare and assess earlier such concerns. Concepts of what constitutes 'special educational needs' in the 1990s have to be understood in relation to key educational developments in the last hundred years or so, especially those which were concerned with the overall raising of standards. As more and more children were included in education, the likelihood of substantial numbers finding learning difficult was strong.

Poverty and Literacy

Research in the 1990s presents findings which link poor socio-economic home background to low levels of achievement in literacy and numeracy. Statistical evidence in the 1920s was rehearsing such findings but with a use of more emotive language than that which most current educational researchers would regard as appropriate. Burt, for example, examined the differences in general ability due to social status, comparing children from two schools in one London borough. The one was composed of families from the highest social status then sending their children to elementary schools. The other was described as being

> . . . in one of the meanest of the overcrowded slums that cluster about the great railway termini. In Charles Booth's map of London poverty the streets from which the latter is recruited are marked as of the lowest types – 'very poor' and 'criminal'. (p. 190)

He found that the 'superior' school was nearly a year ahead of the general average and the 'poor' school more than a year behind. He suggests that 'The backwardness of the "poor" school is likewise most obvious when the children emerge from the infants' department', where he sees the children wearing the imprint of their parents' poverty, a powerful image of social conditioning. He goes on to stress that 'above all things, for children from the lower social strata the harder literary tests must lie for ever beyond their cultural horizon' (p. 192). It seems unlikely that those who research special educational needs in the 1990s would countenance concepts such as a fixed 'cultural horizon'. The comprehensive revolution which profoundly altered secondary schooling in Britain during the latter half of the century was conceived on the premise that children develop at different rates and that all should be given the opportunity to extend and surpass their personal cultural horizons.

In much of the educational literature of the late 1800s and early 1900s there is evidence of a critical evaluation of what are seen as utopian aspirations for children of the poor who are assumed to be unlikely to benefit from anything other than the most rudimentary form of elementary schooling. There is an inference, from several authors, that educating children beyond what is perceived as their 'cultural horizon' can only end in their suffering. An anonymous author (D.L.C., 1878) wrote a tirade on *The Educational Craze and its Results: School Boards, Their extravagance and inefficiency*, in which was said of poor children:

> Can anyone, with the feeblest glimmering of common sense, fail to acknowledge the absurdity of dragging hundreds, not to say thousands, of these miserable objects within the precincts of a schoolroom, to be crammed with indigestible mental food,

that can never be of the smallest service to them in enabling them to earn an honest living? . . . As Mr. Justice Manstry rightly observed, in his charge to the grand jury in Newcastle last July, 'Little good could be expected from educating children during the day, if they have to return to scenes of filth and squalor, of misery and vice at night'. (p. 94)

The notion of the 'undeserving poor' was still embedded in the educational thinking behind such a sentiment, where the author goes on to suggest that the only solution is to send such children to residential training schools, where their home influence is muted. In current debates on rates of literacy in different areas of Britain, it is usually those urban boroughs with high rates of poverty which are seen as the greatest challenge to educators. However, whereas the argument at the beginning of this century was that compulsory elementary schooling for all could involve removing children from their employment where they served as a vital source of income in poor families, by the end of the century staying on in secondary school has become a substitute for work, where post-16 opportunities have evaporated.

Testing Reading Comprehension

It is important to treat any tests with a sceptical critical analysis, recognizing that they are artificial constructions, created in a specific cultural context as a necessarily restricted measuring tool. The Binet–Simon scale, for example, became popular in the 1920s because it provided a practical snapshot instrument to be used by teachers, doctors and social workers, often engrossed with the administration of the Mental Deficiency Acts (Burt, 1922). Current tests for reading comprehension need to be practical and easy to administer if they are to be popular with busy educational psychologists and teachers.

Reading for pleasure, as a popular pastime, was confined to those households which made time and placed value on what, in the mid-1800s, was considered to be a frivolous activity for the wealthy to indulge in. In 1837, the Central Society of Education in London made statistical inquiries into the social conditions of the working classes. They took Marylebone as one of their districts and they presented the following findings related to environmental factors which influenced literacy: of the families visited, 777 parents could read and 267 could not; 343 families had books, 233 had none; of those who had books in the house, they usually totalled a Bible and a Prayer Book; 510 children went to school, 1064 did not; if 500 of those were too young for school, it still left as many not attending school as attending. Their observations about reading levels are interesting. They reported that:

The character of the schools which they attend will be a subject for subsequent inquiry; but the very imperfect manner in which many who professed to be able to read could do so, indicates a state of things of not the highest order. 747 children are returned as being able to read, and 823 as not being able to do so: — it must be borne in mind, that a great number who could but just spell over the words are classed among those who are able to read. (p. 341)

A free school had been established in Westminster in the early 1800s, which used students trained by teachers to teach basic skills and 'religious and moral instruction' (Colquhoun, 1806). If it set a pattern for teaching reading, then it was at a rudimentary level of comprehension. There were eight classes, going from the first class in which pupils learnt the alphabet, a superintending monitor having the letters of the alphabet on pasteboard suspended from his neck. The second class worked on words of two letters, the third on words of three letters, the fourth on words of four letters, the fifth on words of five or more letters. The sixth class reads, in rotation, the Psalter, New Testament, and other appropriate books of instruction, aided by tutors and a superintending monitor. The seventh class reads the Old Testament and the eighth class, which is composed of the best readers, reads portions of Scripture and books which support religion and virtue.

The Elementary Education Act of 1870 which established compulsory education in Board Schools was designed to promote mass education and general literacy. Its critics maintained that it had produced poor-quality 'parrot-drill' learning which did little to raise standards. The reading levels were assessed by school inspectors as poor overall, with scant indication of real comprehension of what was learnt. One Board School pupil, for example, learnt all the capitals of Europe and recited them fairly accurately. When asked by the inspector if they were animals or vegetables, the boy replied 'Hanimals to be sure!', confirming his lack of understanding about what he had learnt by rote.

Cyril Burt probably ranks as one of the most influential psychologists in British educational history, especially as regards his status within the London County Council. His book on *Mental and Scholastic Tests*, published in 1922, was to have a profound influence on intelligence-testing in London and beyond. His attitude towards those who were 'backward' in reading was emphatic. He says that where a child's mental age for reading is little over 80 or 85 per cent of his mental age for intelligence, he will seek his information as an adult from sources other than books. He goes on to say:

> Of those showing a mental age of only 8, barely 12% have continued their reading after they have left school. Below this general level, a servant, a farm hand, or a dock labourer scarcely ever opens the pages of a book or glances at the columns of a newspaper; if he receives a letter, he asks a friend to read it. Accordingly, to teach reading in a special school to children whose mental ratio is less than 50% is simply to squander time and energy. Even with those whose mental ratio falls between 50 and 60%, reading should be limited to grasping the sense of common words and the meaning of brief passages. To work through paragraphs of printed matter is an exercise that should be forced on none but the brightest or the intrinsically gifted. (p. 283)

For special educators in the 1990s, Burt's sentiments are shocking in their conservatism concerning cultural horizons and appropriate limits. It seems important to me that we remind ourselves of where we have come from and how far we have struggled to push the boundaries of what constitutes educability. Drawing upon many diverse ways of teaching children to read, special educators now succed in supporting literacy where, in the recent past, it would have been deemed absurdly utopian. We must always reflect that one generation's utopia can become another generation's challenge.

The Dangers of Raising Standards

In the 1990s' debates on school effectiveness and the drive to raise overall levels of achievement, there is no argument presented which signals the inherent dangers in raising standards (and, correspondingly, expectations). Whilst educational researchers of the 1990s examine the expansion of school exclusions and the problem of truancy, they are unlikely to suggest that mass education is, in itself, dangerous. At the end of the twentieth century there is a global agreement that education is beneficial. It is one of the key measures of a successful country and a central component of competition between cultures. Around the turn of the nineteenth and beginning of the twentieth century, education and literacy in particular was seen by some as a superfluous activity which could easily become subverted into revolutionary thinking. The skill of reading was potentially dangerous, as critics of the Board Schools testified:

> Should the reader feel any desire to know, to what account the 'priceless boon' of reading is turned, to a large extent, at any rate, by those on whom it has been conferred; all that is required, is to cull from the window of the small news-shop nearest to any Board school; specimens of the literature most in demand on Sunday mornings, among the striplings who chance to have spare coins for investment in some of the numerous trashy periodicals of the day.
> A small amount of observation, suffices to show, that in many districts, the majority of printed sheets circulating most freely among the school children, are just those that teem either with the very worst or most mischievous fictions, or with the highly flavoured and barbarously illustrated rakings from the police courts. Some of the narratives of the most nauseous and revolting passing events, are interspersed with sentiments subversive of all respect for authority, law, religion or government, or indeed, for any kind or form of subordination. (D.C.L., p. 138)

The Board Schools were expected to teach moral and religious codes, but the problem with reading is that it cannot be controlled. Once children have acquired the skill, they can use it to subvert the system and to gain access to unsavoury forms of literature. It is interesting that the same is now being said about the Internet, the late twentieth-century form of communication.

Early in this century, IQ testing became very popular and set standards by which a child could be regarded as educable. Testing in elementary schools was used to assess those who would not benefit from an extended school education and who could leave early after basic skills training. This was expressed by Garrett (1928), a School Medical Officer turned barrister, in these terms: 'Of course, there must be a limit, at some point, for the education of any and every child' (p. 74). He went on to say that 'Many illiterates are trade experts of the highest order, and no employer engaging a man to do such work as they do ever dreams of asking a question as to his scholarship' (p. 126). For the early twentieth century, there were considerable dangers in raising standards of literacy. It could lead to expressions of disatisfaction at working conditions, raised expectations and restlessness. The labouring poor were then required to be obedient, easy to train and contented with minimal stimulation and reward. For this, they had employment despite low or non-existent literacy skills. To raise literacy standards was to create potential disharmony and revolt.

The late twentieth century presents a very different picture. More and more children are assessed under legislation, like the 1994 Code of Practice in the UK, as requiring additional support with their literacy and numeracy skills. In a society with high levels of unemployment, a decaying industrial base and minimal requirements for unskilled labour, raising literacy standards is a political expedient rather than mere altruism. The 50 to 60 per cent IQ to which Burt refers would not now deter special educators, as such children are likely to be mainstreamed and receiving additional tuition. It is important to reflect that until the 1971 Education Act, children deemed to have IQs below 60 to 70 per cent were regarded as ineducable. Now children with Down syndrome are being integrated into primary schools and into some secondary schools, taught to read and write, and some are passing national exams and going on to further and higher education. This is where we need to reflect carefully on concepts of 'cultural horizons' and 'limits'.

It is a naïve assumption to equate the passage of time with inevitable progress. In many respects, regression and destruction are more often experienced as innovative ideas are superseded by oppressive legislation. Before I examine some current approaches to the teaching of reading, it is useful to assess where our present concern for raising literacy skills fits into the broader historical perspective, in what ways we have advanced and where we may have created new dangers. When the ferociously critical tracts which greeted mass education under the Elementary Education Act of 1870 are evaluated in the light of developments through the 1990s, it is clear that concepts of 'normal' and 'backward' achievement are relative. Teachers in the 1990s are working with mixed-ability classes among whom there are children who, under early twentieth-century mental-age testing, would be regarded as barely educable. That special educators achieve considerable progress with many of these children by the use of eclectic and imaginative methods is an evident indictment of formerly imposed cultural horizons and a setting of limits.

Where the late twentieth-century impetus to assess, categorize and evaluate needs is fostering potential dangers is in the expansion of a group who are excluded on the grounds of their learning disability and behavioural difficulty. There was much protestation about the unruly and uncivilized behaviour of Board School pupils who were often referred to as 'street ruffians'. Teaching these 'ruffians' to read, write and add up, as well as imposing religious and moral values upon them, was seen by many conservative thinkers in the early 1900s as a radical and revolutionary move to raise the status of the masses. It would be a deep sadness if, in the name of 'raising standards', the late twentieth-century equivalents of 'street ruffians' were thrown back out of compulsory schooling and into street life and potential crime. That is precisely what reformers who campaigned for the Elementary Education Act 1870 were arguing that they wished to rescue such children from. Their expressed sentiments of 'preventing those calamities which lead to idleness and crimes, and produce poverty and misery, by guiding and properly directing the early conduct of the lower orders of the community' (Colquhoun, 1806, p. 11) may now have been replaced by political rhetoric about rights, choices and economic competitors, but the potential dangers remain. A generation of young school drop-outs, despairing of finding any paid employment, are a significant threat to the community, and merely expanding the prison capacity is no answer to their legitimate anger and frustration.

Current Methods of Teaching Reading

One of the most interesting aspects of our global communication in the late twentieth century is that it influences all areas of life, including educational methods. Methods to teach children reading skills have been exchanged from one side of the world to the other, adopted by widely different cultures. Reading Recovery, for example, was started by Marie Clay (1985) in New Zealand in the 1970s. Her approach was characteristic of mainstream education in the Southern hemisphere in reflecting a holistic approach and the priority given to literacy in New Zealand, which involved schools being given large supplies of books. Attempts to apply this method in England and Wales were too short-lived to assess their efficacy, and the current use of this intervention in Scotland is not yet assessed. It is interesting that England and Scotland differ considerably in their concerns for literacy skills, despite their geographical proximity. Scotland largely ignored the debate about 'real books', for example, which was a key issue in England in 1990 (Johnston, 1992), although there has been a continuing concern about meeting the needs of pupils with specific learning difficulties/dyslexia in Scotland. In an attempt to address severe literacy difficulties in mainstream schools, Tayside Region has begun to use 'Reading For Sure' (RFS), a system which originated in Australia. This was developed in private practice by a clinical psychologist from Perth, Western Australia, Dr Julia Soloman, who devised what she called 'diacritical marks'. These are based on international pronunciation marks, including a dot, a stroke or a minute graphic symbol placed above or below the normal printed text. In Australia, this method is used in relatively few schools as yet, as Hellier (1996) discovered on his visit from the UK:

> The application of RFS in Australia has lacked any rigorous evaluation and has progressed through private practice and individual schools whose headteachers have seen value in using it. Given its apparent emphasis on analytical and bottom-up teaching strategies, it has been largely ignored by the establishment in Australia, where global and top-down teaching methods are promoted. This overfocus on holistic strategies appears paradoxical, given the continuing high failure rates in mainstream education across the Australian states (Crawford, 1992). (p. 133)

Tayside has piloted the method in one secondary and its feeder primary schools with a sample of children who were predominantly identified as experiencing specific learning difficulties/dyslexia. Hellier (1996) records that for all children the experience of learning codes appeared to engender a more careful analysis of text and a reduction in inaccurate guessing of whole words. It also allowed them to read material which previously had been impossible for them to attempt.

The increased level of comprehension is clearly significant as is the raised self-esteem. It appears to give children who read slowly by inaccurately using phonic methods a means to develop accuracy. Scotland has long maintained a high reputation for educational excellence, children being given a rich diet of phonics teaching in their early years, which is complementary to the RFS approach. It is interesting that Hellier observes that Scottish children may be better placed than their Australian counterparts to benefit from this method. With much criticism of the transplanting of one teaching approach from one country to another (e.g. from Taiwan to Britain) in order to raise standards, it is pertinent that a method devised in one culture might be more easily used in another very different culture.

It is important to recognize the politics of teaching methods. The recent responses to dyslexia, a growth area in the late twentieth century, have been met with scepticism in many quarters. It is no surprise, therefore, that Hellier reports on the lack of interest in the RFS scheme in mainstream schools which support a holistic approach. For some educators, a focus upon dyslexia equates to an élitist approach to learning difficulties which isolates specific literacy needs and ignores the more general problems of a slow learner.

One of the obstacles to learning to read is the tedium experienced by those children who have to repeat and repeat the same words, without apparent progress. A relatively new method being used in Coventry offers a way of helping children to learn common words with the support of visual and verbal cues, which are personal, specified by the child, with meaning for them. This is clearly appreciated by the children and is far removed from the meaningless rote learning of the early 1900s, where all the children were taught the same sequence of words in stages.

Reflections

Reading is an emotive topic, which polarizes people and in which compromise is difficult. In a recent response to a reported decline in literacy standards, Peter Pumfrey reflected that the least successful readers were now less successful than they used to be. This could be due to many factors, including perhaps an increase in relative poverty for many households in the UK. To paraphrase Brecht, people need bread before they can forge revolution. The link between poverty and reading failure is important to understand in any debate about raising standards. It is noticeable, globally, that where countries are enjoying relative prosperity and expanding their economy, reading standards are higher than the international average. Developing literacy and numeracy skills requires external motivation for most people and, where employment prospects are promising, they have a powerful motivator. In countries where employment opportunities are poor and working conditions severely constrained, there is little incentive to acquire high levels of literacy and, for some governments, the need to retain an available pool of poor and illiterate labourers is integral to the economy.

We can only really assess our current crisis in education in the Western world by reflecting on the last century of developments and change. There are many sceptics who now talk of education having replaced training for young people in countries like the UK. With a dwindling industrial base and mass youth unemployment, young people are being encouraged to stay on at school longer than ever before in history. Theoretically, their literacy and numeracy skills should be better than ever before. In reality, the longer they stay in schools, the longer they remain absent from the unemployment statistics. Any government wishing to maintain or acquire power will use education as a tool. In the rhetoric of 'raising standards' there is an underlying panic about potential revolt on a scale and a level of sophistication never seen in the UK before.

THREE

Addressing Challenging Behaviours: Moral Values and Public Panic

The vexed issue of addressing the needs of young people who are difficult to manage has been a long-term source of disquiet. It is an emotionally fraught minefield, crossed at your peril, for almost any view on behavioural difficulties is fiercely contested. Recognizing the level of passionate debate which this topic engenders, I feel it is foolhardy to pretend to a reasoned objectivity. We are all subjective when examining the behaviour of others, for we can only use our own attitudes as measures. In the way we construct our arguments, select our data and decide on tools of analysis, we are making moral as well as cognitive commitments (Schwandt, 1996). I think it is most important to establish this bias of self-judgement from the outset if the educational researcher and observer is to be truly reflective concerning an issue which is essentially about how we feel — as a society, as an institution and as individuals — when we are challenged by behaviours we find disturbing.

The language used to describe youth behaviour which challenges has altered through the century, shifting from 'delinquent' to 'maladjusted' to 'emotional and behavioural difficulty' to 'challenging'. This semantic sequence may say more about professional delicacy concerning the use of offensive language than reflecting a recognition of fundamental changes in definition. There have always been conflicting views over whether those whose behaviour is disturbing should be described as 'mad' or 'bad'. Whilst professionals are usually reluctant to use terms like 'bad' or 'evil' to describe individuals but will tend to isolate the specific behaviours as negative, the general public has become more vociferous in seeking protection from what the tabloids tell them is a vicious onslaught by aggressive youths. The children who murder, assault and rob old people and deal in drugs are presented as a symbol of the late twentieth-century crisis in moral values and a valid cause of public panic. The picture of an urban jungle where gangs of youngsters own the streets and older people fear leaving their homes at night is one promoted by a press which has become adept at fuelling public panic.

My approach in discussing this area is to examine changing attitudes over the century and their impact on treatment. This reflection will include the influence of a changing society, new demands on institutions and individual perspectives on behaviour which challenges. My hypothesis is that the debates on moral values and public panic which have continued through the century have defined the way in which certain behaviours are seen as challenging.

We need to begin by looking at what was seen as challenging behaviour in young people at different stages of history and in contrasting cultures if we are to evaluate the effect of dominant values on what challenges the status quo. A significant change in moral values alters perceptions of behaviours which are seen to challenge. The behaviour which was seen as challenging in an earlier cultural context is often markedly different from the behaviour which challenges today. What is viewed as appropriate behaviour in one country can be seen as delinquent in another. To a considerable extent, we may be seen to get the anti-social behaviours we deserve and our conception of behaviours which challenge reflects current moral values and public concerns. The late twentieth century may be seen to be largely preoccupied with a prevailing anxiety about social disintegration, especially in the affluent Northern hemisphere. Rising divorce rates, high adult and youth unemployment and decaying industrial bases have threatened the stability of what constituted a structured social framework and we have lost models to emulate. It might be postulated that, as far as Britain is concerned, the loss of empire has led to a fragmented diversity, in which there is no ideal way of life but many disparate choices.

This can be seen to have fostered fragmentation at three levels, from a micro- to a macro-perspective: the self is fragmented, with plural identities and gender differences redefined and deconstructed; the family as an institution and the workplace as an extended family have both been recognized as more fragile, fractured and insecure than previously conceived; a strong economy and a stable society are no longer to be relied upon as frameworks in which to prosper and progress. A climate of social disintegration can be seen to call for a scapegoat or a stigmatized group to vent public distaste, frustration and blaming upon: it requires symbols of degeneracy. Young people have historically been projected as instinctively evil until tamed and it has always been politically expedient to use the tool of public panic to preserve a threatened social stability. The few are punished for the good of the many, adherence to a dominant status quo being of paramount importance in maintaining national cohesion.

Moral Values and Public Panic

I am going to explore the influence of moral values and public panic on behaviours which are seen as challenging in young people by taking three examples of distinct stages of history or contrasting cultural contexts. The first is to go back in European history to child-witch trials in Germany and link this with the current demonization of disruptive children in Britain. The second is to examine perceptions of challenging youth behaviour from the mid-1800s and early 1900s to the present, as educational developments in Britain have constantly changed what counts as morally defective behaviour and what constitutes a decline in standards. The third is to compare the cultural context in the Northern and Southern hemispheres and illustrate that behaviour which challenges the status quo in one context can be seen as appropriate and rational in another. In relation to all three aspects, the concern with social disintegration runs like a connecting thread, indicating why certain behaviours create public panic and a call for 'moral values' to be reinstated.

Children as Devils

After recent murders of children by other children and widespread public fears of an epidemic of unruly behaviour amongst the 'delinquent element' in state schools, it is not fanciful to suggest that there has been a demonization of stigmatized individuals. Through an irresponsible press, these children can be publicly branded as 'evil' before they enter their teenage years. Their adult role is thus allocated to them as that of outsider, feared and hated, an object of contempt.

It seems to me to be no coincidence that the fuelling of public anxiety about delinquency has increased in relation to the developing emphasis on moral values and the need to preserve family, religious conformism and social structures, especially in the last few months from a campaigning and electioneering British government. The need to appeal to middle-class, middle England requires that those who threaten social stability are seen to be treated with firm authority. Thus, the prison population of Britain is to expand to exceed the rest of Europe and to compare with that of the most authoritarian regimes such as those of Malaysia and Thailand.

Punitive measures towards schools which cannot cope can be seen as equally draconian. During a period when legislation has consistently driven schools to compete against each other, those left at the margins through their socio-economic location and past history are allowed to wilt with inadequate resources and a demoralized staff. Thus, a case like the Ridings School in Halifax becomes a prime target for public outrage. The wide publicity given to this untypical situation ensured that many parents were even more convinced than before that they could not trust their children to state schooling where they might be exposed to aggressive and disruptive children. There is often a cry of 'falling standards' whenever politicians wish to stir the public conscience and to focus on convenient scapegoats for electioneering purposes. It is a concept which is highly questionable, as 'standards' in behaviour and academic achievement can only be truly assessed against a broad, historical analysis rather than a short-term reflection. Currently, politicians see the teacher training of the 1960s as the root cause of many present ills. This assumes that what happens in schools and on the streets is all about how teachers are prepared for the job and not about what is happening to society and the cultural shifts which influence the public imagination.

I would like to draw an example from a long way back, as it helps to place our current demonization of children in context. During the 1600s, in early modern Germany, children who were dislocated from conventional society and operating as beggars were branded and punished as child-witches (Walinski-Kiehl, 1988). In Salzburg, from 1675 to 1690, there was a crusade by the prince-bishops against vagrancy as a result of which 56 boys aged from 9 to 16 years were executed. This was a cultural process which involved stigmatizing as deviant those mobile social groups whose lifestyle ran counter to the pious, family-based morality that the élite advocated. The child witch-trials tended to occur at a time when regimes were making concentrated efforts to reform society and to impose new ethics on populations.

Linking a former church-dominated culture to the secular one of late twentieth-century Europe may seem to stretch credulity but I would claim that there are valuable lessons to be drawn. A threat to social stability which is capable of moving the boundaries of cultural definition can create public disquiet and lead to a fragmented and ungovernable plurality. For the 1600s, the church was the voice which influenced the general populace; for the late 1900s, it is more likely to be the popular press and the other media. From the 1950s in Britain, there has been the emergence of a youth culture with teddy-boys, 'mods and rockers' and images of rebellion and dissidence established in the public mind. British newspapers like the *Daily Mirror* and the *Sun* have used recent incidents of disruptive behaviour in schools to foster public anxiety, outrage and reactionary behaviour. They tell of what they describe as 'horror attacks' by very young children on fragile, female teachers and even provide a list of the 40 'worst thugs' in Britain, cataloguing their 'violence' against pupils and teachers (e.g. *Daily Mirror*, 3 October 1996). Referring to young children as 'thugs' is a powerful means of criminalizing their behaviour and taking it out of context into a public trial by media in which individual pupils are ostracized as intrinsically 'bad'. The public are presented with a newspaper impression of violent, wild and vicious children attacking fearful, anxious, innocent teachers.

Exploring the actual context might have led to other stories. Some teachers provoke and verbally torment pupils. The curriculum can be arid and meaningless for some children. Family life may be so fraught that school is the only place where any form of aggression can be expressed. Anna-Marie, for example, the daughter of Fred and Rosemary West, was excluded from school for bullying, which was perhaps her only way of expressing anger at her own constant abuse from her parents (Sounes, 1995). Whilst the Wests were an extreme example, there are other children in schools in the 1990s who experience parental abuse which they are unlikely to confide to their teachers but may express as anger.

Many factors could lead to those incidents baldly stated in the press, like 'Pupil, 11, attacks woman teacher'. Yet, if moral values are to be placed high on the political agenda, it must be seen publicly that delinquent behaviour, which is easily presented to the general public as violence, cannot be tolerated or contained. The emphasis is on eradicating impurities from a culture which has become so pluralist and unequal that it threatens social stability and fosters reactionary attitudes.

Moral Defectives and the Decline in Standards

It is easy for us in the late 1990s, living in countries like Britain and America, to take free state education for granted as a long-established civil right. However, it seems to me to be most important that we do not forget how relatively recent free state education is. The Education Acts of 1870, 1876 and 1880 brought universal, compulsory education to England.

They also meant that children regarded as 'dull' came into compulsory schooling. Pritchard (1963) said:

These children clogged the lower classes of the schools. Children of ten years of age and upwards should have been in Standard IV or higher, yet in 1880 only forty-seven per cent of such children were in the upper standards. Since dull children could gain exemption and leave at the legal minimum age by good attendance over five years, many of them left school without passing beyond or even into Standard III. (p. 116)

The number of children failing to learn the basic skills could be considerable. Pritchard noted that almost every London school had 70 children in Standard I, of whom 25 were not seen to be achieving. As a result, the teachers tended to concentrate on the more capable and to ignore the 25 who learnt nothing and who tended to be disruptive or truant. This was the problem seen to confront School Boards of the late 1800s.

Expectations of the majority of poor children catered for by the Board Schools centred on basic values, with rather less emphasis given to basic skills. In the late 1880s, critics were not afraid of deriding what they perceived as misguided philanthropy from School Boards determined to educate the labouring classes 'above their station' and, thus, to make them discontented with their limited social horizons and frustrated by their struggle in a competitive and hierarchical labour market. In the late 1990s massive youth unemployment, particularly in areas of high socio-economic deprivation and amongst already disadvantaged groups like Afro-Caribbean youths, is rarely alluded to in the public arena as equating to disruption and disaffection in schools, especially by those learners who feel ostracized by the system. We may need to reflect on the original rationale, in many reformer minds, for compulsory schooling and whether it still pertains today.

Educational reformers of the 1880s were concerned to improve the health, hygiene and moral behaviour of the labouring poor (e.g. Colquhoun, 1806; Wyse et al., 1837; Campbell, 1922). They were then, however, expected to know their place and to be prepared for their role within the social hierarchy. By implication, these young people were perceived as morally defective until taught the values of the dominant culture. There was considerable concern expressed that educating 'street ruffians', as they were commonly termed, would lead to trouble in their adult life and in society generally as their increased access into a privileged advancement could not but devalue the experience itself and downgrade all who attended such schooling. As one anonymous critic asked, what was to be the future of the 'prospective careers of the urchins who are being turned out by tens of thousands, in a constant stream, and bearing the brand "Educated" stamped upon them?' (D.C.L., 1878, p. 149). What had been an exclusive label was now threatened with becoming commonplace.

It is useful for British educationalists in the late 1990s to reflect that similar criticisms are now being made of the mass expansion of higher education in the United Kingdom and elsewhere (Corbett and McGinty, 1996). As soon as any form of privilege, including schooling or university education, becomes accessible to those from non-traditional groups (e.g. working-class, black, mature women, learning-disabled) the product itself is devalued. Its status was dependent upon its exclusivity. Interestingly, there could be said to be an increase of challenging behaviour on campus as well as in schools (e.g. Butzer, 1995). Students have more rights than ever before and the new wave of those entering higher education are asserting their rights and protests in an individualistic rather than ideological manner, as befits the late 1990s culture of self-interest. The political protests of the late 1960s reflected a predominantly middle-class student body fired with idealism; those of the late 1990s reflect the pluralistic student body of the new universities, disillusioned with services they perceive as second-rate and unequal. However, if we move away from a Eurocentric or Northern hemisphere perspective, we see that compulsory schooling is not universal and that definitions of those behaviours which challenge are all relative and culturally specific.

Cultural Differences and Behaviours Which Challenge

The media in Britain are perennially preoccupied with the 'youth problem'. This largely concerns young teenagers experimenting with drugs, stealing and causing disturbances in public spaces or, at the most extreme, becoming violent and lawless. There may be seen to be a class bias to this media perception, in that public schoolboys 'scrumping' apples from an orchard may be regarded as a lark, whilst working-class kids stealing fruit from a market stall is seen as a crime. To a disturbing degree, the popular press has consistently fuelled an image of unmanageable young people (predominantly male) who attack their teachers, truant from school, have no respect for authority (be it parental, institutional or state) and are seen as living outside society and its moral codes. The recent cult film *Trainspotting* was a vivid reflection of the Northern European image of 'street youth', and showed an Edinburgh gang stealing to pay for hard drugs, living beyond social norms, rejecting authority and conventional values, anarchic and prepared to use violence to survive. Whilst there may be young people who identify with some aspects of their behaviour and find them to be the late twentieth-century anti-heroes, they are clearly presented as a formidable challenge to social stability and a threat to a fragile status quo as old cultural certainties crumble.

Alongside this call for a return to moral values (assuming that the morality of the past was superior), there has been an increased concern over recent years about children who are 'at risk'. This has created many new networks and support agencies in Britain and elsewhere, which are providing for young people under 16 years old who may be sexually and/or physically abused and those who are homeless in large cities, vulnerable to exploitation. The league of 'caring professionals' from health, social and education services is involved in protecting and guiding young people they perceive as in danger because of their life on the social margins without the support of responsible adults.

There are evident tensions here. On the one hand, there is a concern that in these deconstructed cultures the next generation may contain a significant minority whose anti-social behaviour disrupts an already dangerously fragmented structural cohesion. On the other hand, there is increased social concern for the protection of a vulnerable group who are essentially still regarded as children. This tension, creating an uneasy mix of fear and pity, may be seen to embody the cultural crisis in the Northern hemisphere. For the next generation, their social legacy is one of continued economic instability and fragmentation of families and institutional structures — neither marriage nor the 'old firm' being necessarily 'for life'. They are largely resistant to the old work ethic of the recent past, for it no longer pertains, and with fewer employment opportunities the stigma of the 'dole' has lessened. Whilst traditional concepts of transition to adult status tended to include leaving home and getting a job, there are many young people now who stay in the family home well into their twenties as they are unable or unwilling to find employment and cannot move out. Together with the pattern of more young people staying on at school beyond 16 because there are fewer unskilled jobs or apprenticeships available, the overall effect is to prolong artificially the period of adolescent dependency to an extent not prevalent in earlier generations. The artificial stage of long childhood, created by industrialization in the 1850s, has now become an established structure without the systems which then legitimated it.

However, this prolonged adolescence is not a common feature of the developing world. Arnon Bar-On (1997), from the department of social work at the University of Botswana, has presented a most thoughtful critique of what are reflected as 'Northern, middle-class' (p. 63) attitudes influencing judgements on the lives of street children in parts of Africa. When 13- or 14-year-olds are disruptive in British schools or are found begging in busy shopping centres, they are not regarded as adults but as children. Bar-On suggests that more Northern than Southern societies have gravitated towards a protective model of childhood as a result of many factors which are not part of the experience of most countries in the Southern hemisphere. The lowered birth rate has made children almost a vanishing species in the North. In Europe, children under 15 years old made up only 20 per cent of the population in 1991 and their number is expected to decrease. In Africa, 45 per cent of the population in 1991 was 15 years old or under. Therefore, the South has different priorities to the North. Economically, children in the Northern hemisphere are relatively worthless to their parents but their value is affective and intrinsic. For families in the South, the situation is almost reversed as physical labour is valued, poverty is endemic and welfare systems almost non-existent. Thus, the rational approach is to ensure that children start earning as soon as possible. The increased emphasis on protective care in the North is seen as less relevant within a context of struggle for economic survival.

Bar-On suggests that:

> Northern judgements about children's behaviour and life styles that do not conform to these standards are, therefore, becoming increasingly harsh, whereas for the people of the South, with other agendas, they are simply accepted or at least condoned. (p. 66)

A school curriculum which seems irrelevant to their needs and a pressure to conform at home has often led to African children moving on to the streets. They work at casual tasks like street vending, portering, car-washing, running errands and guarding merchandise. However, not all of those in the working group are abandoned or runaways. Some have homes to return to and make regular contact with their families.

Where they threaten the status quo is in their very visibility. As Bar-On says:

> Their very presence thereby challenges bourgeois society which governs in the

expectation that children will intrude as little as possible on the adult world, and distinguishes sharply between public and private, so generating calls that street children disappear from view. (p. 68)

Far from being physically and emotionally deprived, Bar-On suggests that these children, aged mostly from 13 to 15 years, were able to earn up to one to one and a half times the minimum wage of adults, and were usually well clothed and fed. They also worked and lived in groups. They were generally not committing criminal acts but tended to be most often detained by police in 'clean-up' campaigns prior to tourist seasons. Bar-On suggests that these children learnt many useful lessons from the street, which helped them with leadership, co-operation, social competence, confidence and resourcefulness. Bar-On asks us to reflect that living in the streets may not be so intolerable and dangerous for these children in this context. Yet the dominant European attitude is that such a life is highly undesirable for children under the age of 16. Bar-On challenges our caution by saying that to rely for our knowledge of human maturation on Northern-informed developmental psychology is unhelpful in other cultures. There are parts of the world where children do not remain as children for so long as they do in Britain, but they are able to attain adult status in early adolescence because they learn to adapt to the circumstances which surround them. In this process, they could be seen to have empowered themselves, much to the discomfort of the caring professions who see themselves as the custodians of empowerment.

Children who are displaying adult characteristics of autonomy, economic independence and social awareness can proffer a challenging precocity. That they are not visibly suffering but appear to be contented can be even more disturbing to those who seek to take control of their care. Bar-On reflected that:

The biggest challenge to social policy to ensure the wellbeing of street children . . . is to decriminalise the street. Placing a premium on life organised around formal frameworks and private property, middle-class decision-makers equate the street with idleness, and idleness with delinquency, and consequently construct street life as illegitimate. Two of the oldest measures to this effect are the prohibition of street trading and loitering, that were introduced to the South by its then colonial masters to 'protect' them from 'the natives'. Upheld by the present ruling class for much the same reason, child streetism is thus criminalised automatically, with the result that street children are handled — or more often mishandled — primarily by the punitive arms of the state. Hence, as the children themselves are first to report, their major concern is police harassment, or as one child put it: 'It doesn't matter how you behave [or] what you do, they always see you as a street kid' (Oliveira et al., 1992, p. 170). It is therefore no wonder that the actors most involved in the eradication of child streetism are middle-class community leaders, and individuals like the Aga Khan and Crown Prince Hassan bin Talal who make up the Independent Commission on International Humanitarian Issues. All of these people are undoubtedly sincere, but I would venture to suggest that they are more driven by the fear of street children than by genuine concern for their wellbeing. (pp. 75-6)

In reflecting upon the force of fear as a response to perceived challenges to the dominant culture, Bar-On's observations are redolent of those reasons why child-witches were executed in the 1600s. It is about a fear of behaviours outside social control and, therefore, unmanageable and unpredictable.

Conclusion

Challenging behaviours challenge our mindsets. They disrupt our mental and emotional constructs, making us feel vulnerable, frightened and angry. This is true for the teacher confronted by a hostile pupil. It is also true for any of us who experience challenges which require a major readjustment to our own mental map. Psychologists like Dorothy Rowe remind us to acknowledge the metaphors and myths which we live our lives by when we find ourselves furiously resistant to change.

I have drawn on a diverse range of sources to offer a cultural analysis which moves away from the well-documented classroom- and school-based focus. It is important to consider that societies have often reacted punitively or with extreme anxiety to any indications of youthful revolt. Ensuring that the next generation replicates the values of the last is a way both of preserving the status quo and also of justifying existing patterns of behaviour. Whilst an analysis which relates past behaviours and contrasting cultures to the current British context may seem diffuse, it can provide a sorely needed filter which avoids the knee-jerk reactions of much recent political rhetoric.

From my examination of behaviour which challenges social norms, I suggest that there is a need for a disintegrating culture to create scapegoats. The judgements may come from the church, the media or the caring professions. All three can be dis-empowering, by imposing their own mindsets on what they see as challenging, regardless of how those who challenge may feel. Those parents who were sent to prison by the nineteenth-century British School Boards (D.C.L., 1878) for their children's non-attendance at school protested that they needed the income which the children brought in to provide the basics, as those children were often the sole family bread-winners. This plea may be echoed in parts of Africa at the end of the twentieth century, as Bar-On (1997) illustrates. Children, in such a context, are unlikely to perceive schooling in the same way as those who do not face severe economic hardship. Their streetwise edge is a mechanism for survival, and is not necessarily intended as an affront to those in authority.

As the century lurches to its conclusion there is an intense concentration upon behaviour management, classroom control and behavioural analysis which has extended into British schools. Coping with pupils who have 'emotional and behavioural difficulties' has become a central task of psychological support services, in the urgency to address the current crisis. It can sometimes appear overwhelming and depressingly negative. Applying a cultural analysis does not solve any immediate problems. It can, however, assist in an understanding of why fragmented cultures need scapegoats, and how those who seem to challenge may view their behaviour in a way which differs from how those who find it challenging may perceive it.

FOUR

A Century of Change:
Treatments and Tensions

The twentieth century has seen the influence of medical intervention to prevent childhood disability and the gradual erosion of what has become known as 'the medical model'. It has also been a period in which treatments have been tried and tested, adapted for other purposes or revised. Whilst key developments in medicine and psychology may appear marginal to the area of schooling, constrained as it is by government legislation, they have framed our conception of what signifies as 'special' in education.

Over recent years educational theorists have been concerned with the nature of inclusive education, exploring the degree to which a diverse range of individual needs can realistically be met in a mainstream classroom. One of the oft-repeated maxims has been that 'children don't need integration; they need education'. It is the access to quality education itself which is the primary consideration. This attitude serves to clearly distinguish what may be medical care needs from educational needs. However, the concept of special need is amorphous and has changed considerably through the century. Where it once signified children who were blind, deaf or physically disabled and who attended the early special schools, it now covers a diverse range of learners and keeps adding new syndromes to the list.

There has been a dramatic reversal of what was seen as constituting special educational needs over the century. In the early 1900s, children with physical and sensory disabilities were placed in special schools as a progressive move to acknowledge their specific medical requirements. In the late 1900s, the inclusive education rhetoric has brought many children with physical and sensory disabilities into mainstream education, but an educational culture of selection and competition has systematically excluded those who are disruptive in class and who have difficulties in learning. The redefinition of what constitutes significant special need reflects changes in society and in how schooling is perceived. It has little connection with recognizing individual differences.

In order to examine changes in treatments, concepts and tensions over the century, I shall begin by exploring both negative and positive aspects of medical intervention. This will be further illustrated by examining one example of treatment which influenced special schooling within a socio-economic framework. The importance of medical intervention in parts of the developing world will be assessed in relation to current challenges to the medical model from Western countries. The chapter will conclude with an analysis of where current special education initiatives are framed within models which reflect their cultural priorities.

The Medical Model and its Legacy

When theorists of special education refer to 'the medical model' of disability, it is generally in derogatory terms. They see it as a negative portrayal of an individual whose physical, sensory or intellectual qualities are presented as deficient and abnormal. The focus is upon what is wrong with the body and mind, not on the person themselves as a multi-faceted individual.

I saw a particularly dreadful example of this in the early 1990s in a conference on medical advances in the area of childhood disability. One consultant gave a slide lecture of the dramatic physical improvements he had made on the body of a young woman with spina bifida. He showed the audience slide after slide of the woman's body in its twisted shape and then its progression through each stage of a long sequence of operations. The object of concern had become the body rather than the person inside. He presented the systematic straightening of the spine as a triumph of his surgical intervention. The observers were supposed to be impressed by his prowess, persistence and determination to normalize the deformed body which he saw as a challenge to his professional skills. In an audience composed predominantly of male doctors, I felt angry and embarrassed for this young woman whose adolescent body was exposed to a professional gaze without her individual presence. I wanted to ask her 'Was it worth all the pain of operation after operation to be made "more normal"?' when she was said to continue experiencing great difficulties in walking. 'Does it matter so much that you look different?'

Arguments against the medical model of disability are that it champions a narrow stereotype of normality, rather than fostering a celebration of difference. Another speaker at the same conference presented examples of how children with Down syndrome had their faces operated on to remove traces which marked them out as different. This issue raises perennial tensions in the 'medical model' debate. Some doctors argue that the tongues of many children with Down syndrome prevent them being able to speak properly and that such surgery was therefore not merely cosmetic. Others argued that alterations to eyes and mouth were an assault on the person for purely social reasons, placating parental desires for a child who appeared normal.

To set against negative aspects of the medical model, recent conferences indicate that a real effort is now being made to counterbalance the professional dominance of the past. One, for example (Royal Society of Medicine, November 1996), included people with disabilities as 'Users' Perspectives' at every stage where doctors and other health professionals had expressed their opinions. The influence of the social model of disability is finding its way into medical arenas. This is an approach which rejects the focus on individual deficits, features of a body which need correction, challenging instead the social obstacles which prevent an individual from a full experience of citizenship. At its most extreme, the social model of disability suggests that it is social obstacles *alone* which prevent a disabled individual from enjoying a full life, rather than recognizing that there can be aspects of discomfort, pain, distress, isolation and frustration which are related to the specific disability and are not easily overcome by the simple removal of social obstacles. Presenting a dichotomy between the medical and social models of disability does not necessarily help in a clear understanding of their influence upon special education provision and practice. The medical model is not all bad; the social model is not all good. There are problematic elements of both. It is simplistic to assume that medical intervention always highlights individual deficits without acknowledging social obstacles and attempting to resolve them. If we look back earlier into this century, we can see examples where medical developments have had wide social implications and have improved the overall quality of life for significant numbers of children.

The Case of Tuberculosis

The link between medical progress and the education of children with disabilities is vividly demonstrated in the example of tuberculosis. In the early part of this century, hygiene was a significant problem in the USA as elsewhere, as Myers (1970) recalls: 'I taught in a rural school in the year 1907-08, where all the children and the teacher used a single tin cup to dip and drink water from a common pail' (p. 4). Disease was quickly spread and tuberculosis was a critical problem. In 1921 Myers established a school for tuberculous children at Lymanhurst where students were taught, given additional food and an afternoon rest hour. A lamp was found which gave ultraviolet rays in the same proportion as those in Alpine sunlight and it was incorporated into the daily programme. In addition, space on the roof of the building, when climatic conditions permitted, provided natural sunlight therapy. This offers a good example of an early special school for 'delicate' children. In 1935 it was closed to become a diagnostic and epidemiologic centre, reflecting the complex relationship that exists between medical research and special education practice.

It may be difficult for special education theorists of the late 1990s to see medical intervention as anything other than conservative in concept, yet early in this century new approaches to preventative medicine were seen by some as a form of radical social engineering. Teller (1988) recalls how:

> In America some children were temporarily placed in preventoria; the first preven-torium was opened in Lakewood, New Jersey, in 1909 but some moved to Farmingdale in that state because of strong local opposition, climaxing in the arrest of the superintendent on the charge of bringing indigent children into the state. The Farmingdale preventorium accepted children from the homes of poor consump-tives; they stayed at the institute from three to six months. The youngsters enjoyed life in the open air and abundant meals; they were taught cleanliness and hygiene as well as regular school subjects. During a child's stay at the preventorium efforts were made to send the tuberculous family member to a sanatorium and improve the sanitary and hygienic conditions of the home. By 1916 there were eight preventoria in the USA with the room for about 300 children. (p. 110)

The relationship between poverty and illness was clearly recognized and was reflected in the nature of special schooling. It can be said that in the Northern hemisphere generally, where material living conditions have steadily improved overall during the last hundred years, diseases of poverty, malnutrition and unhygienic practices have been considerably reduced. However, this reflects neither areas of dire poverty in affluent countries nor the current conditions of many developing countries.

Millard (1996) records the current rise in the incidence of tuberculosis in poor areas of the UK and the USA. In Eastern Europe and the former Soviet Union rates are even higher. These countries lack the resources and skills to control tuberculosis and the interaction between AIDS and tuberculosis presents a grave problem. As in the beginning of the twentieth century, there is evidence that an increase in tuberculosis is closely correlated with gross overcrowding, as in areas like the Bronx, Liverpool and London. Unlike some other modern diseases, tuberculosis has become a low-profile disease which is under-funded, despite its increasing prevalence among people whose resistance has been lowered by HIV and AIDS. The current epidemic of tuberculosis in New York is occurring among the most neglected members of society.

We cannot consider children with special educational, social and health needs at the end of the twentieth century without confronting the current and perennial social diseases which serve as demarcation zones which give some such unequal chances against others. Speaking of the cruel legacy of AIDS in children entering the twenty-first century, Matsaniotis (1996), a professor of paediatrics at the University of Athens, says:

> Never has it been more obvious that social injustice, poor health, disease and inadequate treatment of disease in one part of the globe may place in great danger other persons in other places be they wealthy and educated or poor and ignorant. (p. 323)

He reflects that the tragic irony of AIDS is that its results aggravate the socio-economic circumstances which facilitate its spread, and reminds us that for the next fifteen years AIDS will be one of the major killers of children. It might legitimately be said that, whilst tuberculosis was the major killer disease at the beginning of the twentieth century, it is AIDS which has taken its place at the century's end. Barnes (1995) saw tuberculosis as a social disease and, in researching its effect in nineteenth-century France, saw it as a social signifier of decay and revolt. The gradual bodily decay and languish meant that tuberculosis gave spiritual redemption a material shape. In 1906, a cartoon in the French journal *La Voix du Peuple* (*Voice of the People*) showed a sick man alongside a healthy one. The sick one had the caption, '10 hours, long days, breed the seed of tuberculosis'; the healthy one, '8 hours, short days, seeds of revolt' (Barnes, 1995, p. 216). The metaphors of decay and repressed revolt are powerful social images of subtle and insidious control.

There are evident tensions in any current academic debates which seek crudely to polarize social models of disability at one end of the spectrum and medical models at the other. Medicine has always been about social conditions and there is much documentation of the ways in which medical intervention has sought to engage in social engineering to improve health and quality of life prospects for the poorest in society. The case of tuberculosis offers a valuable early twentieth-century example of this and AIDS a chilling end-of-the-century example. AIDS is not just about adult gay men, as the popular Northern hemisphere image tends to project. If we are to consider children with special educational, social and health needs in a global context, we must look to countries like Africa where the incidence of infection is 40 times higher than in Europe and 20 times than in the USA. Part of the special educational needs of children in countries like Africa is to be well informed about safe sex in carefully delivered sex education programmes. Matsaniotis (1996) suggests that the threat of AIDS leaves no alternative and that the use of young volunteers would be most valuable. He suggests three basic survival factors: better schooling, quality media and improved primary health care. His emphasis is of interest to me, in reflecting on the cultural context of special educational needs. 'Schooling' can only be seen as one element, not as the key component of any effective support service. In placing media effectiveness alongside health and educational services, Matsaniotis is clearly committed to a holistic and comprehensive interpretation of special need. Factors are complex and multi-faceted, one resource having implications for another. Individual differences require a collaborative and complementary system of support structures and available resources which can accommodate diverse experiences.

Tensions in the Social Model of Disability

In my earlier reference in this chapter to the social model of disability, I suggested that the most extreme forms of analysis could place social and economic obstacles alone as the oppressive factors in the lives of disabled people whilst disregarding individual life experiences. The impetus to accentuate the positive and to produce forceful images of solidarity is characteristic of many subcultures seeking to define their collective identity. Disability culture is following a pattern, well established by other oppressed groups, of minimizing individual differences in order to maximize collaboration and cohesion. However, the tensions within this subculture reflect those in society at large. Some women, for example, feel that their views are ignored and that a macho culture pervades the disability movement. A few even feel bullied into submissive silence by a dominant discourse of social model values which equate individual expressions of pain or distress with weakness and disloyalty to the movement.

My perception is that the disability movement in Britain is following that of America into a more confident and assertive stage of its development after the initial anger and drive for unity. It is at this second stage that the opportunity for expression of individual differences can flourish. Among several disabled women in particular, the call for an inclusion of the 'personal as political' in the social model discourse is constantly heard. It has generated tensions. Individual differences may produce conflicting accounts of experiences of disability and different perceptions of social barriers. Yet I would contend that it has also produced a human face on an otherwise potentially distancing presentation. In their most intense and unpalatable forms, both the medical and social models of disability are inhumane and unacceptably detached. The medical stance can present the doctor as godlike and autocratic, viewing the disabled person as a body only, with no interest or concern for the person inside.

Similarly, a rigid adherence to a social model can address broad economic, political and social issues only, with no interest or concern for personal needs and feelings.

In an interesting analysis of feminist philosophical reflections on disability, Susan Wendell (1996), an Associate Professor of Women's Studies at Simon Fraser University in British Columbia, suggests that the increased pace of living in the Northern hemisphere has socially constructed an increase in incidents of disability. If what is seen as 'normal' becomes being high-pressured and being driven to increased productivity, this will lead to more people becoming disabled by stress, exhaustion and anxiety. Alongside the cultural factors which create a disabling society, Wendell cautions that notions of everyone being disabled to some degree can underestimate the significantly different experiences of people with severe and long-term disabilities. Her own experience of ME (myalgic encephalomyelitis) has given her a first-hand demonstration of the limits of empathy, as her intense pain and physical restrictions are sometimes referred to by others as symptoms of the tiredness and stress they often feel. Like AIDS, the disease of ME could be symbolized as a cultural feature of late twentieth-century spiritual malaise, reflecting a weary depression in a driven and anxious social maze. Where radical changes in Eastern Europe, China and Russia have now dissolved familiar boundaries, they have also created acute cultural chaos and a crisis of spiritual identity.

Unless there is a recognition of personal, cultural and locational differences which influence the ways in which disability is experienced, the medical and social models will offer limited scope for effective use in any analysis beyond the most elementary level. It is valuable, I believe, to consider the specific stages of development reached by different cultures in relation to conceptions of disability. Just as in countries like Britain and America a social model may be at a sophisticated level of development after moving through its earlier, raw stages, so the medical model may be at a basic social engineering and intervention stage in parts of the developing world. It is important for us in the Northern hemisphere to consider the extent to which our concern with disability politics is relevant and useful to those who are still struggling with widespread disease and malnutrition in the developing world.

The Developing World and Medical Intervention

Within global power differentials, it is the United States and Western Europe which tend to provide and instil their dominant models of health, education and social service provision in the developing world. By inference, that substantial section of the world which is still seen as lagging behind the technological and economic advances of the Northern hemisphere is regarded as in need of help and advice if it is to grow to a more sophisticated level. Whilst it is all too easy to condemn the traditional authorities of medical and social welfare provision as imposing colonial models of care onto developing countries, it is rather more uncomfortable for radical ideologists to recognize that it can be their social models and child-centred concern which may create cultural dissonance.

In a powerful critique of cultural imperialism in South Asia, in which disability development is seen by Western planners in terms of human rights and community-based rehabilitation regardless of the actual strengths and weaknesses of the communities, Miles (1996) suggests that extending information, knowledge and skills is more vital within this context than the promotion of disability politics. A campaign to eradicate polio displays some of the difficulties. It needs a radical improvement in health care among poorer South Asians. It also requires a degree of autonomy which is alien to a culture lacking the level of individual-orientation common to Western conceptions of self. The contrast between the analysis of disability presented by a Canadian philosopher like Wendell (1996) and the issues given priority in South Asia could not be more marked. Miles reminds us that a poor family in rural Asia, given a prognosis that their severely disabled infant will be dependent for life, may well decide to let the child die for the well-being of the rest of the family.

Miles refers in his analysis to the 'promotion of criticism-struggle' by Western social scientists as:

. . . a luxury affordable in western Europe, i.e. in societies that have begun to function with historically unprecedented levels of interconnectedness, public trust and cooperation. The latter factors have begun to be prized, and their fragility recognised, as the bleakness of purely market-driven futures becomes apparent. Yet the socio-political diseases of South Asia are the 'disconnections' of caste and of the endemic mistrust towards anyone to whom one is not closely related. These add greatly to the time and energy costs of doing everything, whether buying a rail ticket, planning an accessible school or motivating groups of disabled people. Such diseases are probably reinforced by western sociological imperialism wherein the efforts of health and rehabilitation workers past and present are rubbished by airconditioned journalists and ivory-tower social scientists, seldom having personal experience of disability service planning and delivery. (Miles, 1996, pp. 495-6)

This is angry polemic and could be regarded as a jibe at those Westerners who earn their livings and academic reputations from aligning themselves to disability politics and anti-discrimination campaigning. Yet it is also a warning against the blanket transfer of cultural ideologies from one context into a very different one. Improved basic health care information is vital in many areas of the developing world, as literature promoted by various charitable organizations indicates, e.g. *Let's Learn about Acute Respiratory Infections: How to Recognise and Treat Pneumonia at First-level Health Facilities* (AHRTAG, Working for Health Worldwide, 1995); *New Move to Wipe out Polio* (British Overseas Development, 1996). In the journal for the Uganda Society for Disabled Children (USDC, 1995), a positive and culturally sensitive approach to training is promoted. The training programme uses 'facilitators' as volunteers living in the community who have shown sensitivity to people with disabilities. They may be parents of a disabled child or be disabled themselves. They give encouragement to carers and to disabled people and raise awareness of disability at a village level. Local artisans, like carpenters, blacksmiths and cobblers, are trained to produce and maintain simple, low-cost rehabilitation aids and appliances, which is of critical importance in poor, rural economies. In the 1994/95 financial year in Uganda, the training extended to 140 facilitators in each district, 423 government staff at district level and at least one

Organisation of People with Disabilities in each district.

These figures give a valuable insight into different priority needs in different areas of the world. It seems to me to be appropriate and culturally comfortable that Western European and American values are person-centred, entitlement-focused and concerned with individual needs. This fits squarely into a familiarity with capitalist values and the rights of the individual in a competitive society. Within this conceptual framework, the disability civil rights movement follows other civil rights initiatives as a call for social inclusion and positive, valued identities in a pluralistic culture. If we are immersed in a 'me' culture, then we all want to be included. Within this culture, disabled sociologists focus their analysis upon the inequities of social barriers and the importance of fostering positive individual identities through the support structures of collective solidarity in disability politics. It seems absolutely right for these sentiments and priorities to be promoted in an area of the world which has become used to privileged health, education and social services, albeit a world which now experiences widening gaps between rich and poor.

However, I would argue that it can become an arrogant gesture to assume that other cultures need, or ought, to place the same level of priority on social equality issues. It requires a significant channelling of emotional and physical energy to become actively angry for collective rights and to advocate for individual needs and wants. Where many of the population are starving and weakened by disease, basic needs supersede those of a more complex, cerebral nature. It is not to imply that social inequalities and stigmatized individual identities should remain unchallenged. Rather, I would argue that priorities are culturally specific, and models of what seems most appropriate at the current time will vary according to locational circumstances. Unless immediate, urgent priorities are firstly addressed, the more politically sensitive awareness-raising is unlikely to take hold in the general imagination.

In Chapter 3, I cited Bar-On's (1997) analysis of street children in Africa as challenging Northern hemisphere concepts of childhood. An organization called Children of the Andes seeks to 'rescue, protect and rehabilitate the lost children of Columbia'. Their medical intervention includes providing young leukaemia patients with 'total care for children from poor rural families during their stay in the capital for treatment' (*Newsletter*, 1996, p. 2). This level of social and medical intervention is redolent of that discussed earlier in this chapter, provided by the preventoria in America and through Western Europe in the early 1900s, to help children from poor families who had tuberculosis. It is a complex and potentially uneasy mixture of preventative medicine and social engineering. Applying Bar-On's cultural analysis, can street life in Accra or Bogotá be readily associated with street life in London or New York? The social frameworks are conceptually dichotomous and it means something fundamentally different to be a 13-year-old living on the streets in London compared to a 13-year-old living on the streets in Bogotá. Again, it might be useful to apply the 'priority issues' analysis which I found helpful in examining the global adoption of a social model of disability. In a cultural context where there are many competing and urgent basic priorities and where violence and social instability are endemic, the degree to which street children are regarded as tragic victims is likely to be dissipated. They are but one reflection of their cultural context and they may have opted for the streets in preference to alternatives, as Bar-On implied and as the 'Children of the Andes' Rescue Patrols found in the response from some children, who said they did not like the children's homes they had experienced as an alternative to sleeping rough.

Tensions exist where boundaries of understanding are threatened. In the Northern hemisphere, it has involved disability-rights activists rejecting and challenging the service-providers and charities who felt they were working in their best interests. In the Southern hemisphere, it has involved a discomfort of differences relating to priority of needs and conceptions of individual versus community rights, as aid workers either inadvertently or deliberately impose their values on another culture.

In an interesting analysis of the effects of the Bosnian war upon disabled children, Hastie (1997) demonstrates that the social model can be received favourably within a culture which still embraces the medical model, if the circumstances are such that change is inevitable. She found that the war, dreadful as it was, presented a tremendous opportunity for social change. Institutions and services had collapsed and people were looking to other countries for support. It was a time for the disability movement to gain ground in a situation where disabled people were usually taken care of by others without negotiation as to their needs. Out of tragedy grew the chance for new ways of presenting care and treatment.

The Implications for the Twenty-first Century

Despite a rhetoric of inclusion, special education continues to reflect medical and psychological concepts of what constitutes a disabling condition. The expansion of the social model of disability in the United States and Western Europe has led to challenges both to the dominance of the medical model and to the preservation of a special, segregated system. Priorities of need differ in countries where preventative medical intervention is required to confront diseases which are rarely found in the Northern hemisphere. The AIDS epidemic affects both the developing world and other parts of the globe and has significant implications for children growing up in the early part of the twenty-first century. The complex relationship between social exclusion, stigmatized diseases and socio-economic cycles of deprivation creates tensions within current ideological frameworks which attempt to conceptualize disability.

It may no longer be helpful to us, moving into the twenty-first century, to present contrasting images of the medical versus the social model of disability; we need to find other metaphors to encapsulate a complex, interconnected and rapidly changing global network. At one extreme, Wendell (1996) refers to illnesses not existing unless doctors label them. At another, Yuan (1996) compares Michael Jackson, the Afro-American pop celebrity, to the Elephant Man in his bodily strangeness and use of public spectacle to acquire 'freak' status. With reference to parts of the developing world, Miles (1996) suggests that some people experience ways of life two hundred years removed from the late 1990s technological revolution.

Special education is about conceptualizing and then responding to disability. A metaphor for the individual-focused Western world might be that of a hand grasping money from a central pile; for the developing world, that of a sea of hands reaching towards the elusive source of funds. Special education in the West is about individual entitlement; in other areas, it relates more to mass need. Entitlement and need are different concepts and produce different labelling processes.

In the next chapter, the notion of illnesses not existing unless doctors label them will be extended in a debate on special education labelling throughout the twentieth century and its impact on current assessment and provision. The differential status of various labels will be compared and the wide discrepancies between an 'entitlement' curriculum and a response to urgent needs discussed within an international perspective. The cultural status of different disability labels conveys comfort to many parents and recipients of services whilst helping to foster a hierarchy of acceptable and unacceptable special educational needs.

FIVE

Values, Choice and Entitlement

Introduction

If we acknowledge that behaviours which challenge the status quo are culturally specific and that priorities on the disability rights agenda vary according to what are seen as urgent issues in a particular context, then we are recognizing the centrality of values in any debate on special educational needs. The term 'values' is employed so frequently by politicians and the church in respect of educational priorities that it has ceased to hold the clarity of definition which it might have had in a more homogeneous society.

In this chapter the key issues to be explored involve nebulous and ambiguous concepts, often exploited and colonized by those with their own personal agendas. In relation to notions of 'values', it is asking what is valued and who is valued. Unless we explore this approach, the status of special education is not contextualized in the broader, judgemental framework of what sceptics refer to as 'the real world'. The chapter will then address the relationship between choice and entitlement and the difference between entitlement and need. These are not mere philosophical concepts but are fundamental to an understanding of the development of special education through the latter part of the twentieth century. The chapter will conclude with an analysis of the tensions between an individualistic approach to entitlement and a community approach to need.

Values and Cultural Capital

When people talk of values, especially when they are politicians, they often mean to present a superficial appearance of taking the high moral ground. It is an emotive word and, consequently, one regarded with deep suspicion by many. In the area of schooling, Lawton (1997) suggests that terms like values, beliefs, attitudes and expectations tend to be used as if they all exist at the same level of consciousness. He recommends that different levels be recognized, behaviour being part of the surface culture of schools, fundamental beliefs being part of the deep cultural structure, with attitudes and values existing somewhere in between the surface and deep cultures. I find his analysis helpful, in that it places values within a complex interrelatedness which acknowledges different levels of awareness. There are those who espouse one set of values, yet operate within another. They may not recognize the ambiguity, so deeply embedded are their attitudes. It is because our values influence our behaviour that we need to relate them to the ways in which we prioritize in our daily lives.

Special educators and related professionals are as prone to prejudice as anyone else, even if they feel that their work affords them a special insight. An example from recent history is the case of Dr Langdon Down, superintendent at Normansfield Hospital, Middlesex from 1858 until 1868 and known especially for his work on ethnology, Down syndrome being his most famous work of classification. In a recent analysis of his impact, the renowned special educator Wolf Wolfensberger suggested that Langdon Down was the victim of a kind of hoax in which the culture that produced Darwinism and eugenics was also influenced by the travelling fairs of the late nineteenth century (Crowhurst, 1996). The *Völkerschau* involved the exhibiting of strange people considered to be exotic in form or manner. When Langdon Down observed that members of one race could acquire the characteristics of another, he went on to coin the term 'mongolism' and also applied a new classification, the Aztec type, to people with microcephaly. Wolfensberger indicates that his so-called scientific judgements were based on deeply ingrained and familiar patterns of prejudice, which assumed the following: that races are unequal and hierarchical; that members of a particular ethnic group look alike; that members of the 'lower races' are childlike; that acquired characteristics can be inherited; that mentality is correlated with personal appearance and can be 'read' from it. The influence of popular culture (the exhibiting of exotic freaks in the travelling fairs) upon scientific objectivity is important to consider. Where values are layered elements within cultural identity, it can be extremely difficult for those professing objective classification to distinguish between their own perceptions and their professional analysis. Where certain subcultures have low cultural capital, as did those who were exhibited as freaks of nature, they are likely to be assessed as unworthy of humane treatment on the grounds that their social contribution is minimal and their level of dependency excessive. It seems important to me that we recognize the relationship between popular culture and so-called professional objectivity, for no individual is free from the cultural influences which surround them. Our perceptions of those whom educators and related professionals deem to be especially needy are fundamentally linked to our historical stage, cultural context and place within the hierarchy.

Taking the example of Langdon Down as a nineteenth-century prejudice and one which special educators in the late 1990s would seek to resist at all costs, it is interesting to note that some dilemmas can now arise in relation to values and the move towards increased political correctness. This is a relatively recent phenomenon, imported to Western Europe from North America, in which heightened sensitivity towards minorities is viewed as a positive and necessary form of anti-discrimination. Whilst this movement has led to many positive practices and enhanced awareness of the power of language to empower rather than alienate vulnerable people, it has sometimes led to tensions between competing value systems. Kendall (1996) offers an interesting example from American schooling, in which her wish to place value on other cultures is in conflict with her feelings that children need support in learning how to value others. A 4-year-old boy from a Middle Eastern culture was berating and hitting his mother at the child-care centre in which Kendall was working. She realized that in his culture this behaviour was acceptable because of the inferior status of women. She also knew that, had he been white and middle-class, she would have intervened. She felt that it was important to tell him that in the United States most people do not think it is all right for a child to hit his mother. In this way, she felt that children could be helped to become bicultural and, through this, to develop the skills to thrive in their own culture and in the dominant culture as well. I like the concept of being 'bicultural' and feel it can have a wider application than the example offered here. For people with disabilities, they need to learn to thrive in the dominant culture by gaining access to sources of influence and knowing how and where to get what they need. They also will find support and positive role models within their own subculture which affirms their experiences and perceptions as equal but different.

In an interesting analysis of the use of cultural identity as a potential cure for mental ill-health, Santiago-Irizarry (1996) suggests that cultural sensitivity towards Hispanic groups in American mental health services can assist in the progress towards a bicultural identity. Briggs (1996) indicates that in the relationship between the scholar and the subjects being studied, it is necessary to reinvent the tradition which has informed the authority within that area and to construct it afresh from the perspective of those who are its subjects. Such a stance accords with the American commitment for political correctness but does not recognize the differential power relations which give more listening space to some voices rather than others. In any debate on values, it is vital to be honest about the way some people are more highly valued than others and that gender, class, ethnicity, disability and social status will determine the degree of community response there is to individual need.

Amartya Sen (1981) coined a very thoughtful phrase related to levels of entitlement which he called 'E-mapping'. This concept emerged during the Sahel famines in the 1970s when, although there was enough food to go round, some people starved. Sen concluded that the fact that those people starved was a reflection of their entitlement to resources, what he termed their 'E-mapping'. Following this line of analysis, we may conclude that there are enough resources in our society to provide people with learning disabilities with an improved quality of life but their entitlement is restricted at three levels: structurally, through the economy of services; interactionally, through family overprotectedness and a general disability orientation; and in the expectations of the individuals themselves (Ramcharan *et al.*, 1997).

Within a climate where resources are linked to cultural capital, in other words where entitlement has to be demonstrably presented as necessary, there are bound to be those whose 'E-mapping' is restricted and who will, therefore, lose out. People create their E-maps by structural, interactional and personal means. This requires a high level of cultural awareness and a considerable investment in the stakeholders' society where cultural capital is all important. Choice and the currency of labels relating to degrees of special educational need can better be understood if seen in terms of E-mapping.

Choice and the Currency of Labels

It is important not to perceive concepts like 'entitlement' as value-free elements of fundamental justice. Just as there is the law and the legal process on the one hand and justice on the other (in other words, legal judgments are often neither fair nor just), so there is entitlement to special educational services on the one hand and a fair division of resources on the other. Taking the model of E-mapping as a useful analytical tool, I shall explore the structural, interactional and personal ways in which entitlement is won.

At a structural level, Local Education Authorities (LEAs) in Britain are financially constrained by the limits of their annual special education budget. Whilst they may wish to please all parents who request special resources in theory, they are bound to disappoint some in practice. LEAs are becoming increasingly influenced by advocacy and campaigning groups of parents and professionals. This may be seen as a threatening and potentially divisive development (Bowers, 1996; Gross, 1996). It might, however, be promoted as a sign of healthy individual, rights-led entitlement and an active demonstration of stakeholders claiming their social needs in a competitive culture (Simmons, 1996).

A special education director in a culturally diverse London borough, speaking in a seminar in March 1997, selected the label of 'dyslexia' as one which displayed many of the tensions existing in an entitlement culture. It had become a label which parents did not mind being given to their child and one which often carried substantial resource gains. I shall use this example as a current British feature of special education legislation, by E-mapping the dyslexia tribunals in relation to structural, interactional and personal issues. Special education tribunals have become a recent development from the 1994 Education Act, in which parents have the right to appeal against the placement or degree of resources offered to them by the LEA.

Structurally, the LEA is operating on a budget which should be shared as equitably as possible in relation to the LEA special needs audit. In this, a picture emerges of the level of special educational need which is found overall in the borough, charting the range of needs and levels of specific difficulty. Dyslexia will be only one small element of this overall mapping exercise, by far the majority of learners with special educational needs fitting in to the much broader category of 'moderate learning difficulties'. By the time the LEA is facing parents at the tribunal where their offer of resources is being contested, they will probably already have been engaged in a long-running dispute over the nature or severity of the child's difficulties. Whilst the LEA will be using evidence from their special educational needs audit, mapped out on the stages of the Code of Practice, the tribunal is likely to overrule a locally standardized audit and to suggest that the schools should be doing more than they are able to do.

Interactionally, there is a basic inequity between the relative power and legal force reflected within the professional status of the independent educational psychologists, employed by the parents for the tribunal, and the educational psychologists who form part of the LEA service. In dyslexia cases, the independent educational psychologists will carry out elaborate assessments using arcane test batteries to produce 'block-buster' reports with tabulations, numbers and percentiles. Using this, they will make spurious connections of the test data which reinforce the notion of 'in-child' deficits by highlighting the lower scores on the tests. Often this leads to recommendations which the LEA could not possible meet and to requests, as a result of this, for independent special schooling. Some of the independent educational psychologists act as recruiting agents for independent special schools for children with dyslexia, which have proliferated during the late 1990s in Britain. In contrast to the very thorough preparation and investigation which the independent educational psychologist has been able to conduct, the LEA educational psychologist will be coping with many other demands and, therefore, producing a report which will probably lack the detail, expansiveness and quality which the independent report offers. The LEA assessment will be based on their audit system, which evaluates a continuum of need within that specific LEA context. For example, in the context of a multicultural, metropolitan borough, there may be many children who require additional needs which assume priority over the needs of the minority with the label of dyslexia. The LEA educational psychologist may well feel uncomfortable with labels which distinguish one form of reading difficulty from another and may find the term 'dyslexia' unhelpful. Yet, in the forum of the tribunal, they are forced back to the old psychometric tests in order to compete with the independent educational psychologists. In this interaction, the independent EP will most likely interpret the test data quite differently from the way in which the LEA EP interprets them. As the LEA EP is so aware of the fact that there are many children within the LEA special needs audit who have similar needs which should qualify them for additional support, this may make them vulnerable to the charge that they do not identify all of the child in question's needs in the specific and thorough way in which the independent EP does on behalf of the parents.

Individually, parents will differ considerably in their capacity to gain a successful result on entitlement. For those with campaigning groups to back them, they can be strengthened by past cases and strategic planning. For others who are unfamiliar with the language of professionals (special educators, psychologists and lawyers), the whole process of pursuing a grievance to a tribunal court may seem far too daunting. There have been more tribunals in certain areas of Britain than in others (e.g. suburban South rather than rural North) and a rise in statementing in London which amounts to a twofold increase in three years. The Code of Practice, along with the Parent's Charter, has fostered an individually driven culture in which the clamour for assessment equates with a demand for placement, irrespective of broader community needs and restrictions.

Dyslexia, as a choice of label, offers an interesting example of E-mapping in action. Structurally, there are many demands upon limited LEA resources which all compete for the same communal pot. Single-issue lobbying on behalf of particular disabilities has become a feature of the late 1990s, as parent power has gained in strength. The first challenge in the E-mapping process is to demonstrate to the LEA that your entitlement is of higher priority than that of others and that, unless you are satisfied, you will pursue matters as far as the law will allow. The unequal status in court of the independent EP compared to the LEA EP leads to the next stage of E-mapping. If parents are to be successful in gaining their entitlement, they need to ensure the services of a powerful, independent EP who knows how to convince the listeners that the child's deficits are such that only segregated, residential special schooling of the highest quality will suffice. More parents are now asking for segregated special schooling rather than inclusive education, under the late 1990s British tribunal system

(Advisory Council for Education, 1996). This may seem to be ironic when the impetus used to be for parents to seek mainstream placement for their child with special educational needs. It is a reflection of the individual, entitlement culture in Britain where concern and disquiet about the quality of state education generally has led more parents to express interest in private schooling. The tribunal system can offer an opportunity to gain expensive, private education for those who are able to prove their entitlement worthiness. This leaves many with less clearly and forcefully defined claims in their E-mapping to manage with the little which remains. To return to the image of Sen's (1981) famine, within tribunal E-mapping there appear to be some who feast whilst many are starved of the most basic services through unequal distribution under an entitlement and choice economy.

Values and Inclusive Education

In Chapter 4, I suggested that some developing countries might be so preoccupied with the struggle for basic improvements in preventative medical care that the more ideological and abstract issues associated with disability politics become of secondary importance. This argument also runs true in relation to degrees of inclusiveness within educational provision in different countries. Mazurek and Winzer (1994) have made interesting comparisons between levels of inclusiveness in education throughout the world, ranging from that which is described variously as 'limited', 'emerging', 'segregated', 'approaching' and, finally, 'integrated'. Within that which is 'limited', they reflect that:

> looming social concerns such as solving structural economic problems, providing universal elementary education, and establishing basic health services overshadow the pressing needs of a small and by definition politically and socially disadvantaged special needs minority. (p. 3)

Such a reflection reminds us that values are influenced by contextual factors. In countries where the majority are disadvantaged, there may not be the cultural space for expressing the level of compassion which other, more privileged countries can offer. A relatively recent example of the tension which this can generate was in the exposure of institutional neglect of disabled children in Romania during the late 1980s.

British disability charities had gone out to teach and guide staff in these institutions in how to stimulate disabled children who had been left in primitive conditions. Whilst this was clearly against basic humanitarian values, at one level, and needed to be addressed as a civil rights issue, it also happened to reflect the primitive living conditions beyond the institutions and throughout the depressed economy of the country. The plight of disabled children was bleak but, then, so was the plight of many Romanian citizens. Their apparent indifference to the suffering of these children is surely a reflection of their cultural distress and despair, and British disability charities come with entirely different cultural values, based on a welfare structure which is alien and, in this context, quite lavish. The television documentary which exposed these Romanian institutions illustrated the tensions between local care staff and British charity visitors. Some of the local staff expressed anger that their best efforts were seen as inadequate by these outsiders. Again, I would return to Brecht's maxim that people need bread before they can engage in revolution. Both the care staff and the children needed food and basic needs attended to before they could begin to revolutionize their practice. The hierarchy of values which places primitive needs before more abstract concepts pertains here. Helping the children to be more contented by playing with them was a luxury in a context where just keeping them alive seemed remarkable.

In war zones, attitudes towards disability are influenced by crisis-led value systems. In the West Bank and Gaza Strip, there has been an increase in the number of children with disabilities due to injuries in conflict and also to emotional trauma. In addition, Mazurek and Winzer (1994) suggest that the high percentage of children with cerebral palsy in Nablus, Hebron, Gaza Strip and Ramallah could be due to the fact that inter-marriage and early marriage are more common there than in other areas of the country.

One of the key factors, for me, to emerge from their comparative research is that labelling of disabling conditions is significantly different in the more economically poor countries when compared with the affluent Northern hemisphere. In the West Bank and Gaza Strip, for example, all children with learning disabilities are labelled as 'mentally retarded' and all those with physical disabilities as 'physically disabled'. There are none of the range of labels for behaviour disorder which proliferate in the USA, Australia and the UK. Unless a label is validated, there are no assessments and resources made available. So, in the market-driven cultures, labels become of extreme importance and their cultural capital is substantial.

Entitlement, Labelling and Need

E-mapping plays a central role in choices about special education and in the labels which are applied to specific conditions. There are certain social situations in which entitlement to a label and the resources which accompany it are not the first priority. In areas of the world where childhood disability is created by preventable illnesses and by tropical diseases like leprosy and where civil wars continue to disable young people, concepts of 'choice' and 'entitlement' are ambiguous. The fact that vaccination is widely available in affluent areas of the world, to the extent that it is taken for granted as a human right, means that the available choices are very different to those in the developing world. Urgent campaigns to confront preventable diseases and disabilities create a culture in which health, social and educational rehabilitation takes priority over nuances of inclusive education and this leads to simple and generic labelling (Mazurek and Winzer, 1994). Where priorities are to address basic needs of food, clean water and shelter, the labelling is confined to broad categories of physical and developmental disability and special education may be focused upon practical aids rather than specialist programmes. Entitlement is a concept which can only be measured in relation to what is available and what is perceived as a right in that context. Where the general population overall is given limited choices, it is not surprising that this will also be relevant for children with special educational needs. To apply Maslow's theory of value hierarchies, until basic needs are addressed it is difficult to prioritize individual aspects of emotional, aesthetic and spiritual well-being. My observation is that different societies choose different labels for special needs and use these labels in ways which reflect their cultural values. Countries like the USA, Australia and Britain have created an individualized culture in which self-awareness, self-fulfilment and self-help are concepts to be treated with respect and even reverence. It might be postulated that worship of self has taken the place of the church among many people in these cultures as a new and flourishing religion. This value system has major implications for the labelling of special needs. Rather than applying the broad, generic categories used by many poorer economies, these self-focused countries have created new labels and used these labels to demonstrate entitlement to resources. Taking two labels of the twentieth century — 'autism' and 'attention deficit hyperactivity disorder' — I shall discuss each as it relates to the cultural context from which it emerged.

Autism

Autism is a condition first described by Leo Kanner in 1943. It was defined as a brain disorder which affects the capacity to communicate and he perceived it as a breakdown in affective functioning which left the child isolated and unable to relate to others. In his original paper describing the characteristic features, Kanner suggested that autistic children had an inability to establish social relations, a failure to use language to communicate, an obsessive desire for sameness, a fascination with objects, and had good cognitive potential. After this diagnosis, it was familiar in the 1950s to present a view of autism as being influenced by cold, emotionless parenting, referred to by Kanner as 'refrigerator parenting'. In recent years, there has been much debate about the different degrees and forms of autism which can be assessed and the 'classic' autistic child, as defined by Kanner, is perceived as fairly rare (Trevarthen *et al.*, 1996). Asperger's syndrome, for example, was first defined by Asperger in 1944, a year after Kanner's definition, and has become better known in recent years as more children are diagnosed as having this particular form of autistic behaviour. They are seen to have many of the features of autism but to show no significant delay in their cognitive functioning. There are debates as to whether they can be seen as the same as those with high-functioning autism and the extent to which they reflect stages in a continuum of impairment relating to autism. In their research, Trevarthen *et al.* (1996) observed that Asperger's syndrome is by far the most widespread of the autistic spectrum disorders and that their international comparison figures were based on the assumption that children with autism and related conditions will have the same life expectancy as the general population — an unlikely assumption, as in countries where medical management is less advanced there will be low numbers of children who survive with autism.

I suggest that the progress of the autism label through the latter half of the twentieth century tells us much about our cultural values. The suggestion of cold parenting (for which, read 'mothering') came at a stage of social history when women had been working outside the home during the Second World War and had gained a degree of social and economic independence. Psychiatrists were not the only representatives of conservative opinion to blame them if their children appeared to be unable to communicate, suggesting that mothers' place was in the home and not away from their babies. Alongside the blaming culture there has developed the impetus for labels which define precise and specific brain damage, which points to medical rather than educational causes of disability. Asperger's syndrome has become a sought-after label, as it indicates a type of autism which carries no stigma of learning disability. In developing countries in which rates of infant survival can create a situation where unless infants learn to demand food, attention and protection they may be overlooked, those who live until later childhood with the label of autism may be few in number. Where there are many other factors causing disability, autism may not carry the currency it does in a more affluent culture.

I am not suggesting that children with autism do not have very real problems nor that their parents do not require considerable help. I have worked in two different schools for autistic children in the 1970s and was able to observe the communication challenges at first hand. However, the two schools were so very different and dealt with such disparate needs that they vividly reflected the widely spaced stages along the broad continuum of what constitutes autistic conditions. One school was highly selective, taking only those children who might now be diagnosed as having Asperger's syndrome, whilst the other took any children who were thrown out of other schools. All these children had in common was their overall label. Some (predominantly in the selective school) were able to read, write and cope with arithmetic to examination level. Others (predominantly in the non-selective) were non-verbal and highly destructive. The selective school had a high proportion of children from affluent and professional homes. The non-selective school had a high proportion of children from poor, Afro-Caribbean, working-class homes. That there are many different versions of the same label was clearly illustrated in these contrasting educational settings. This difference is even more pertinent in the contrasting cultures of the Northern and Southern hemispheres. Bar-On (1997) demonstrated that street life for teenagers in Africa may not be seen as disadvantaged in the way it is seen in Western Europe, where a protective psychological model dominates. Similarly, where there is an individualized culture operating, labels like autism are powerfully loaded with a sense of the self; where community values are paramount, those labels which explore concepts of self are less likely to be applied when group needs compete.

Attention deficit hyperactivity disorder

Children now referred to as having attention deficit hyperactivity disorder were labelled earlier this century as having minimal brain dysfunction. An epidemic of encephalitis (inflammation of the brain) in the USA in the early 1900s left many with problems of inattention, impulsivity and hyperactivity.

This label continued until the 1950s and 1960s. The *Diagnostic and Statistical Manual* of 1968 referred to children with hyperkinetic behaviour and this term was applied during the 1960s and 1970s. In 1980, attention deficit disorder became the new label because some researchers felt that inattention was the key element. The 1994 version of the *Diagnostic and Statistical Manual* used the category 'Attention Deficit Hyperactivity Disorder (ADHD)' to include types who were primarily inattentive or primarily hyperactive. Current research in America reflects that ADHD is partially hereditary and not caused by brain damage but by factors in the central nervous system (Wodrich, 1994). It is also seen not to be caused by inappropriate parenting although there is increased emphasis upon the need for consistent parenting in its treatment. Like the label 'autism', ADHD carries the dilemma of a tension between blaming parents for their child's dysfunction or medicalizing the condition totally. Slee, who has observed the rapid increase of the use of the ADHD label in Australia, says that:

> The medicalization of student behaviour transforms others', as well as self, perceptions and, consequently, the status of students. Previously naughty, the ADDS (Attention Deficit Disorder Syndrome) students are qualitatively different. Theirs is a dysfunctional or impaired physiology in need of close specialized attention, generally beyond the scope and qualifications of the regular classroom teacher. The trade-off for the parents, however, is quite beguiling. Used to having their child seen as 'bad', the status of impaired is often preferred . . . ADDS transforms the child from bad to sick. They have an impairment which is not their fault; concomitantly it is not the product of bad parenting. (Slee, 1995, p. 75)

In this analysis, Slee distinguishes those features of labelling which characterize an individualized culture. Within the Australian context, the ADDS label provides a medical status which separates out this individual from all others except those who possess the same label and which absolves parents from all responsibility for fostering the behaviours in any way. They are then entitled to medical resources which will offer a controlling medication to modify their child's behaviour and to educational services to assist their child in managing their behaviour at school. Within a cultural climate in the USA, Australia and the UK which is becoming increasingly concerned with individual responsibility and withdrawal of welfare support, the need for medical labels could be seen as critical. That dysfunctional behaviour might be a feature of disintegrating social structures is another element in the growth of this label, defining a sick rather than a bad society.

Conclusion: E-Mapping and the Charting of Needs

Earlier in this chapter I described the experience of tribunals where dyslexia was the label and where independent educational psychologists were arguing for resources to respond to the needs inherent in the label. With all three of the labels referred to in this chapter, the number of children and young people being diagnosed has expanded over recent years. This has developed alongside an increased interest in the conditions themselves and a high profile being given to these disabilities in countries like the USA, Australia and the UK.

If the incidence of dyslexia among students in higher education is taken as an example of this expansion and increased interest, the power of labelling for cultural capital can be vividly demonstrated. Where post-compulsory education offers a more interesting example than compulsory schooling is that it is dealing with the direct consumers of services, students, rather than with the indirect consumers, parents. Students are now apparently happy to place labels of dyslexia on themselves in countries like the UK and will also self-refer as 'learning disabled' in the USA. There might be several influencing factors. One is that an increasing emphasis on the neuro-logical causes of autism, ADHD, dyslexia and minor learning disabilities offers a biological reason for behaviours and difficulties which absolve the individual from responsibility. Another factor is that the group influence of the disability movement in these countries has made many individuals more assertive about claiming a disabled identity. It no longer carries a negative stigma where it is seen as neurological damage which can be confronted with drugs, programmes and intensive therapy. It fits into the self-help and self-nurturing culture which has gained increasing credence as inner spiritual cleansing has replaced formal religions. Perhaps the most significant factor influencing self-referral is that diagnosis can, and usually does, lead to a rich entitlement to privileged services.

Special education is bound up with value judgements. As ardent inclusive education advocates maintain, if all learners are to be offered inclusive provision they need to be given equal value, regardless of their range of talents and skills. This kind of equity is challenged by the nature of entitlement as it relates to E-mapping. Here, each individual has to prove their personal value in order to gain the right to resources. It is not about sharing out equally, according to need, as Sen (1981) noted. E-mapping requires an elaborate charting of needs (as demonstrated in the dyslexia tribunal procedures) which can illustrate why one specific individual is worthy of their rightful claim, regardless of how inequitable that might be within the totality of general needs. Equity is based on community values; entitlement is about individual values. The labels used in many developing countries still reflect a community concept of need within broad and non-specific categories. Here, labels like ADHD and dyslexia may seem irrelevant, expressing as they do very individualized notions of what can be observed and assessed within much broader categories of need.

If we acknowledge that the Northern hemisphere reflects a culture of individual rather than community values and that entitlement and cultural capital are bound up with values based on self-focused definitions, the dilemma of community care becomes apparent. People with disabilities and learning difficulties are increasingly being cared for within the community rather than in large institutions, yet a community based on individualized values is not conducive to their long-term emotional growth. Within an E-mapping analysis, their stakes in the community are weak and fragile and claims to entitlement are unlikely to be effective unless a climate of community rather than individual values is actively promoted.

In the next chapter, the concept of 'community' will be explored as it relates to E mapping and equity. Student entitlement in further and higher education will be examined, within the institutional community of college and university. The politics of the disability movement will be evaluated as it concerns developments in the disability civil rights community. Dilemmas in the care in the community initiative will be discussed as they relate to notions of choice and empowerment. It is difficult to understand what empowerment means in the field of special education and special provision if it is not firstly contextualized within an entitlement and equity debate.

SIX

Community and the Culture of Caring

Introduction

The way in which individuals are valued determines their status in any community. Wolfensberger, the American guru of 'normalization' (the supporting and training of people with learning difficulties to become sufficiently 'normal' to pass within their community), recognized the importance of valuing individuals in his use of the term 'social role valorization'. The British advocacy campaigning group Values into Action further promotes the concept of value determining status and quality of life.

As the debate on E-mapping in Chapter 5 illustrated, people are not equally valued by their respective communities and they therefore receive inequitable levels of support. Entitlement to services is an equality rhetoric but, as part of a consumer-led impetus, it is a market concept. Knowledge is power and without an astute awareness of how to work the system, entitlement is an elusive value. As a market concept, entitlement to special education services and community provision is more likely to be demonstrated in operation in the Northern hemisphere than in the Southern, where competition for scant resources is much greater and where notions of individual entitlement are unfamiliar.

In exploring the responses of communities to issues relating to disability and special educational needs and to the role of disability culture in that process, I have chosen to focus upon initiatives in the United States of America. This is because the politicization of disability concerns is more highly developed there than in most other countries, following as it does on other campaigning civil rights movements. It is therefore a useful example of a community advocacy and campaigning initiative which has made a significant difference to provision through the force of legislation and policy.

Alongside the major emphasis on American community developments, there will be comparisons made with the United Kingdom, France, the Netherlands, China, Hungary and Israel. It is important to consider what the term 'community' means in different cultures. A community where the needs and wants of individuals are of paramount concern will differ significantly in its value systems from a community where individual wants are subsumed under general needs. The historical attitudes to disability within each culture will affect how children with special educational needs are being valued at the end of the twentieth century and how this influences the ways in which their parents may treat them.

In this chapter I shall explore what a caring community might consist of in late twentieth-century America. Examples will be selected from mainstream community initiatives, from school and university communities and from disability culture. These aspects of community — within mainstream culture, institutional culture and subcultures — are distinctive, yet offer similarities. Each separate cultural climate creates its own dominant value systems, its own routines and rituals and its own conceptual mapping structures of perceiving normality. These climatic influences determine the status quo — be it conventional or subversive — and direct the way in which those who are different will be treated.

Models of caring communities: USA

The ways in which communities respond to their most vulnerable members vary considerably and do not necessarily reflect the benefits of increased education, wealth and technological advance. Often, it is the simple societies which are effective at caring, whilst the more sophisticated forget how to care. In a most thoughtful and reflective analysis of caring in the community, the American psychotherapist and former director of community services for disabled people in Pennsylvania, David Schwartz (1997), assesses the reasons why he feels that professional care in the advanced societies of the Northern hemisphere is so inadequate a substitute for the care given in simpler communities by friends and relatives.

He noted that, even when people were being moved out of large institutions to live in small group homes or in their own homes in the community, they were very often being cared for by others who were paid to be there. He gives examples of local people who, on being asked if they would help a disabled member of their community, in addition to the paid help they received, expressed anxiety that they lacked the skills, and said they would prefer to donate money instead. This reflects the late twentieth-century community malaise in the Western world. We have become dislocated from one another as we frantically pursue our individual goals. The concept of profession-alism has so categorized 'expertise' that ordinary human interactions lack spontaneity when people fear they neither understand nor can respond to the needs of others who are different from themselves.

Schwartz provides a fascinating example of community caring from friends. When a nuclear family was having intense difficulties with a son or daughter who had psychiatric problems, the family therapist who was supporting them asked them to invite up to 70 people into their home in a gathering. At this meeting, the therapist told them that they were a tribe, a facet of community life now lost in late twentieth-century white America. He encouraged them to chant, dance and express their raw feelings. From this activity would often emerge suggestions and offers of support which avoided merely handing over the 'case' to professionals. He called this 'retribalization' and suggested that it still existed beneath the surface of modern life. Cultural analysts may well protest that North America has treated those who preserve tribalism (e.g. the American Indians) with utter contempt and cruelty and that any attempt to imply that a return to tribalism will energize and strengthen the materialistic and individualistic society of rich Americans will be greeted with mocking derision.

Schwartz defines culture as 'what people create if left to their own devices' (p. 83). One central element of this is the capacity for hospitality, in the sense of providing and sustaining care and support for others, including strangers and those who are disabled and in need of extra protection. He suggests that we, as a society, need to re-evaluate what we see as our fundamental beliefs if we are effectively to alter our habitual routines and rituals of caring in the community. This involves confronting and challenging our beliefs in these three certainties: the scarcity of care; the value of the nuclear family as the central source of caring; the notion that formalized service systems are the key response to human need. For the modern, urban and technological community to become more truly hospitable, there needs to be a high value placed upon neighbourly caring rather than reliance upon professional 'wisdom'.

I find Schwartz's arguments persuasive and exciting but fear that the redistributions of responsibility and rights which such changes would necessitate will be hard to establish. Recently, in June 1997, I came upon an interesting example of 'tribalism' which illustrates the difficulties inherent in our current social structures. There are some parents with learning disabilities who find themselves carefully observed and monitored by the 'caring professionals', especially if their children are seen as being at risk of neglect or injury. Clearly, at an objective level, this is important to preserve and the public would be outraged if the children of such parents were in danger because their parents had been left unsupervised. Our feelings are not objective, however, and we bring our prejudices with us to our observations. I was told, by a researcher, that social workers were most unhappy with the fact that this couple crowded their home with lots of friends who also had learning disabilities. The professionals felt that this was a bad influence on the children who did not have learning disabilities. There are two ways of looking at this situation: the parents could be encouraged to enjoy their tribe which offered support, positive identity and solidarity; they could be discouraged from having the people they had selected and replace them with those selected by the professionals in order to offer suitable stimulation. Both could be justified but my bet would be that it would be the professional voices, speaking with the persuasive language of reasonable authority, who would win the argument hands down. For the kind of caring community which Schwartz presents to find favour in the new millennium, there is a need for current care systems to be reassessed in the light of consumer values and for a multiplicity of approaches to be considered as potentially viable. Within our current hierarchies of care agencies, such a procedure will only come about if (as seems to be threatened in Britain at present) health service structures deteriorate to such an extent that community hospitality is urgently required to replace redundant services.

Caring education communities

It is interesting to use the USA as an example of a country where civil rights legislation has influenced the quality of community for disabled students in schools, colleges and universities. Kerzner Lipsky and Gartner (1997) have explored the topic of inclusion and school reform in America and draw conclusions related to preparation for the twenty-first century. They see inclusion in schools as being about a sense of belonging and about the valuing of difference, recognizing that this requires considerable changes in the 'tracking' of students into ability bands which is so prevalent in American schools. The enduring tension in American history, they contest, has been the balance between the many and the one. They say that:

> Inclusive education in restructured schools not only provides benefits for all students but also serves as an exemplar for an inclusive society, one that is diverse and democratic. As alienation threatens community, inclusive education is the seedbed in which we learn to nurture and live in a democratic society. (p. 258)

Their sentiments complement Schwartz's vision of a hospitable community and indicate the social role of schooling as a preparation for an improved future society.

Among the initiatives displayed in American schools and colleges are those of positive discrimination for disadvantaged students, curriculum reform which affirms their experiences and innovative programmes which include even the most severely disabled learners. Ford (1996) has researched the reasons why gifted black students often underachieve in American schools. She suggests that they can challenge teachers by using language and asking direct questions which annoy the teacher and by displaying thinking skills which are unfamiliar and, therefore, disconcerting. She stresses ways in which their learning styles are often distinctive:

> In general, black students prefer to respond with gestalts rather than atomistic responses; they prefer inferential reasoning to deductive or inductive reasoning; they focus on people rather than things; they have a keen sense of justice and are quick to analyze perceived injustices; they lean towards altruism; they prefer novel approaches and freedom (particularly relative to music, clothing, speaking); and they favor nonverbal communication modalities. (p. 15)

Critics may suggest that her analysis reflects a stereotype of black Americans, yet it is refreshing to receive such a description of common features in relation to high levels of intellectual ability rather than in relation to deviance or low performance. What she does emphasize in her research is the need to ensure that gifted black students are not so alienated by their school experience that they underachieve rather than perform to their maximum potential. Recognition and valuing of difference means accepting that there are different ways to be clever as well as different reasons for school failure.

Part of creating an inclusive school community involves the valuing of student experiences and forms of expression. So often, in the past, the dominant modes of communication in schools have marginalized those learners who are unfamiliar with the language and confused by the terms employed. Smith Livdahl *et al.* (1995) brought together a group of English-language teachers from North Dakota and Minnesota to foster and develop what they called 'response-centered' teaching approaches. This approach involved recognizing the constructive elements to learning, which necessitated a constant reformulation of conceptual frameworks, the significance of language in this process and the social context in which learning occurs. The classroom becomes a caring community which supports many views. As one of the team of teachers said:

I try to acknowledge my class as a community of learners and to encourage others to reinforce the risk-taking that occurs in this atmosphere. I remind the curious that this is a process that helps to create able learners from students who may have opted out of the learning process, encourages those who may have been too timid to participate in the risks of active learning, and affirms those who may have been leaders in the classroom, maybe even forcing those leaders to participate at a deeper, more meaningful level. (p. 84)

The image which is created by this presentation of good practice is of a harmonious and caring classroom community, in which students share their strengths with others in an altruistic manner. It is important to reflect that these aspirations and commitment to inclusive practices are operating within a school system which places very young children in special classes in mainstream schools and where violent disaffection among some older students has transformed some 'downtown' problem schools into virtual prisons, with armed guards on the gates. It is, perhaps, symptomatic of a troubled society of the haves and have-nots that idealism amongst some teachers will serve as a counterbalance to the unpalatable realities of much schooling.

An interesting reflection of the wide-reaching effects of a civil rights approach to education in America is that adult programmes now include those with the most complex and multiple disabilities. Giordano (1996), in assessing the literacy needs of adults with learning disabilities, suggests that providing 'compensatory programs' for people with severe and complex disabilities can be too limiting for them. These forms of stimuli often involve the use of light and sound displays designed to stimulate interest and general awareness. He suggests instead that the use of community-based instruction is preferable because it is directed at community inclusion, participation and empowerment and gets people out of segregated spaces into a less restrictive learning environment. Using pictures and labelling in the environment, the claim is that this offers stimuli which surround the person in their daily settings and can thus be generalized in a way in which the segregated programme cannot. What I find most encouraging about this attitude is not that the pre-literacy training in itself may be of direct and immediate benefit but that there should be a concern expressed that allocating specific learners to a highly restrictive setting designed to meet their very special needs is being challenged. There will be conflicting views on such an initiative: some carers may feel that light and sound stimuli in a protective space is just what is needed; others may feel that a pre-literacy experience in the community setting is far more inclusive; yet others may feel that a bit of both is the ideal. What is significant is that those previously hidden away in their community are being encouraged to participate in it as active learners and potential communicators.

At the Saskatchewan Institute of Applied Science and Technology a guidebook has been published for staff and faculty which says:

The first step in dealing with students with disabilities seems obvious: treat them simply as students. They come to SIAST for the same reasons other students do and they bring with them the same range of intelligence and scholastic skills.

It goes on to confront the impact of staff prejudice by saying that negative attitudes can be highly destructive to the student:

> They reduce expectations of the individual's performance. They define the person by the disability, as if it comprises the entirety of his or her being. They lead us to isolate and segregate the disabled, hurt their pride and damage their confidence. The wrong attitudes can be more disabling than any handicap. (SIAST, 1995, p. 2)

The handbook goes on to elaborate upon what constitutes a learning disability and how to respond to these students. In many respects, it can be seen as a most supportive text which promotes a caring educational community. Yet the language it uses (i.e. 'the disabled' and 'handicap') would probably be criticized by disability rights activists who want a more proud and assertive use of terms in any printed documents, even those which support the inclusion of disabled students.

Disability Culture USA

Disability culture is about a sense of community, both an exclusively disabled one and a full participation in the broad community. It can be said to have been born and generated from the USA. Calling for an exclusively disabled community, at one extreme, are disabled activists like Gaspari (1995) who seek a ghetto for disabled people, for 'as miserable as ghettos have been historically, they have often been havens affording a degree of control and incubators for the building of political and economic control for the future' (p. 17). Like many other disempowered minorities, there are those within the disabled community who seek the solidarity that a selective subculture can offer. At another extreme, the disability civil rights movement has long fought for full inclusion. The group ADAPT became the first organization in history to shut down both the Democratic and Republican national headquarters on Tuesday 3 May 1994. This was to protest against health service moves to support death with dignity for disabled people in institutions, rather than to offer them life in their own homes. The journal *Mouth: The Voice of Disability Rights* (1994) states that:

> The average adult who becomes quadriplegic has a better than 90% likelihood of being discharged from the hospital to a nursing home. The life expectancy of a quad in a nursing home is 18 months. If they don't drop you on your head or slam you with the wrong meds, the bedsores will eat you alive. (p. 8)

The journal protests that ADAPT is fighting for every American's right to die free. The campaigning stance is clearly evocative of Schwartz's (1997) plea for a more caring community which enables disabled people to die in their own homes and be supported by friends and neighbours rather than by professional carers. Paid care is cheaper to provide in institutions and paid community carers are unlikely to be as adaptable as friends. Disability activists seek parity with other people who can enjoy living in the community as of right without being made to feel that they are a burden.

The twentieth century has seen the emancipation of disabled people in the USA and many other countries, as they have fought for equality of opportunity. One of the pioneers of the American Disability Movement is Ed Roberts (1939–95), who went to Berkeley University despite being severely physically disabled and who went on, in the spring of 1970, to acquire campus housing for himself and other disabled students, which became the beginning of the Independent Living Movement. From that first Center for Independent Living (CIL), there were over 25 established across the United States by 1977, inspired by and modelled on the CIL at Berkeley. The Americans with Disabilities Act (ADA) was passed in 1990 and has helped to create a vast grassroots self-advocacy movement of disabled activists.

Woodward (1995), reflecting on his work as a member of staff in a CIL, suggests that CILs struggle to remain in touch with grassroot attitudes, feelings and needs whilst at the same time operating as viable and well-organized service-delivery outlets. This tension can generate conflicting feelings among self-advocates who see those who run the CILs as betraying their commitment to disability rights in their urgency to acquire funding and to be seen as worthy among local benefactors. All too easily this can lead them to protect the status quo and to fear challenges which might offend or promote discomfort. It is a perennial dilemma amongst disability charities and any organizations which rely upon public goodwill and the support of wealthy benefactors. As Sue Ralph and I argued in our paper on the changing imagery of charity advertising, using the British charity Mencap as an example, there are considerable tensions between the need to sell an image which attracts financial support and to campaign for equal rights and dignity (Corbett and Ralph, 1994). It is because competing priorities can be prevalent within the agendas of the professional carers in institutions, community services and bureaucratic systems that disabled people and those marginalized by poverty and social stigma can be confronted by professional stereotyping even before they meet with public prejudice.

Caring Communities: International Comparisons

I shall begin this analysis of caring communities by looking at bureaucratic systems in three Northern European countries, England, France and the Netherlands, and the ways in which these countries respond to the needs of the most deprived young people within inner urban communities. I shall then explore concepts of community and the implications of these for assessing the needs of children who are below average in school attainment in China, and of adults with disabilities in Hungary. The final discussion will be around the institution of the family and what disability means to some parents in Israel. Within these three themes of systems, communities and institutions (all elements of the formal and informal network of support and constraint), some international comparisons will be drawn which can serve to illustrate the complexity of defining community values.

(1) Systems which care

In a recent research report (Yarnit, 1997), conducted in Sheffield Education

Department, three inner cities were compared in their efforts to rescue and address inner-city educational crisis. The report author, Martin Yarnit, concluded that Birmingham, the English city in the project, had much to learn from the French city Lille, and the Netherlands city Rotterdam. The area of Lille called Roubaix is regarded by many as the most serious inner-city crisis in France. Its secondary schools compare with the most formidable American examples. Yartin says of one example in Roubaix:

> A grim three-metre high electronic fence surrounds the College Albert Samain, a cordon sanitaire against the drugs and violence of its run-down neighbourhood. Once inside the school, the key message of the principal and his staff was about what had to be done to enable its overwhelmingly North African, Turkish and refugee population to achieve their best. 'But first we must listen, because we cannot expect the children to learn if they are troubled.' (p. 4)

This community ghetto reflects the British context in which the most run-down city schools tend to be those with high populations of refugee and ethnic minority children. Such a school situation can compound their experience of public prejudice with a struggle against institutional apathy and despair, as teachers either leave and the pupils experience a series of supply teachers, or they set their expectations so low that low levels of achievement become a self-fulfilling prophecy. It is all too often the case that, confronted with this scenario, regional resource systems accept the inevitability of 'sink' schools and focus energies on the schools which are seen to work well.

In Lille, the bureaucratic systems have provided a framework which supports community regeneration in a practical and productive way. At the College Albert Samain there are not only supplementary teachers to run its after-school study centre and to offer tuition in French, maths and science, but the college also has a community liaison officer, a nurse and a doctor. These are funded through the Contrat de Ville, which is a contract between central government and France's most disadvantaged urban areas, offering funding in return for achieving clearly stated objectives for housing, jobs, the environment and education. The other element of this system is the creation of *zones d'éducation prioritaire* which provide additional resources to small groups of schools which are required, as their part of the commitment, to deliver a joint development plan showing how they will raise achievement through involving parents and the community. The government set a target for the year 2000 of 80 per cent achieving the *baccalauréat,* and the rate achieved for 1995 was 63 per cent, more than doubling the 24 per cent of 1975 and twice as many as those who currently qualify for university in Britain. The linking of schooling with community, health and social welfare is central to this positive process. For children who are disadvantaged at several levels, their academic achievements are unlikely to be raised without addressing their overall well-being.

They have tried to confront this in Rotterdam where their scheme, DeltaPlan, offers a concerted approach to children and young people's well-being which draws on the combined resources of schools and city health services. Alongside this is the coalition of school boards, linking with a community school to use experiences of difference as a source of learning. In Rotterdam they have used additional funding to make a difference both to individual pupil achievement and to reviving the inner city, providing that clear objectives are established and built into school development plans. This approach is also the one which has placed Birmingham at the centre of the school effectiveness debate in England. The dilemma for Birmingham is that the key sources of urban regeneration funding on which it draws were never designed with education in mind. Yarnit (1997) perceives three main aspects which make its funding unsuitable: it cannot be used for mainstream funding to turn around failing schools; it demands matched funding; it is subject to competition. If the new British government is to extend its commitment to Education Action Zones, this may mean redesigning its systems for urban regeneration to place education at the centre. Inclusive education, if it is to offer real support and recognition of differences, must collate the services of education, health and social systems to provide a caring community inside and beyond the institutional boundaries.

(2) Community caring and community values

The rhetoric of 'effective' schooling and 'high achievement' among pupils, which has become part of the fabric of British educational policy, pays scant attention to deep cultural differences in expectations of individual children. In Chapter 3, I discussed the analysis offered by the African researcher, Bar-On (1997), which suggested that in parts of the world where parents had many children there was likely to be less emphasis on school achievement and individual development than in parts where parents had few children. Where parents have a great deal invested in their children, at an affective level rather than a material level particularly, they often want them to achieve and to compete as an extension of their own feelings of self-worth.

In an interesting debate on dilemmas in curriculum reform in schools in Beijing, Xiaopeng Li (1997) suggests that there is high parental pressure upon children to succeed. Since the one-child policy of the early 1980s, these parents place all their hopes on the one child. Historically, attitudes have changed towards the value of learning. Since the late 1970s there has been criticism of the political movements of the 1960s and early 1970s which devalued knowledge. An effect of social and economic reforms since the early 1980s has been that people in China are now attaching great importance to knowledge and to education. Traditional Chinese values on parenting are that children should be encouraged to become scholars rather than to do other trades. Recent educational policy has been to develop all-round learning in schools but the actual school practice is to reduce the subjects to be examined and to focus upon them. Xiaopeng Li suggests there is a tension between high parental expectations and extremely limited places in senior secondary schools and universities. Within this scenario, what counts as failure or underachievement may be seen as artificially constructed where political values (to produce a balanced workforce) and parental aspirations (that their one child becomes a scholar) are in conflict. The cultural context of underachievement has to be understood if the creation of 'special needs' categories is to be truly evaluated. What is educational failure in one country may be educational success in another. The political history has to be considered as a reason why parents may prioritize certain skills over others: no learning is value-free nor detached from the historical baggage which surrounds it.

Bánfalvy (1996) conducted an empirical study in 1995 in Hungary which took a random sample of about 1300 adults with learning difficulties, who had attended special schooling, from all over Hungary. They collected data from 569 people with mild, 476 with severe and 90 people with very severe learning difficulties. They wanted to explore the quality of life experienced by these people and to identify their unmet needs which should have been provided by special educators and other services. Their aim was to find ways to help this group to become more integrated into the community.

What Bánfalvy considered to be perhaps the most important finding of the research was that life performance and quality of life do not necessarily run parallel. I found the conclusions most reflective when they suggested that:

In spite of the better opportunities for active and social everyday life provided by families with highly educated parents, the self-esteem, the emotional well-being and the social integration of the adults with learning difficulties is better in 'simple' environments compared to the 'high requirement' environments. In fact, those living in 'lower-class' families and those living in villages are better integrated into the surrounding 'normal society' compared to those from the affluent urban middle-class.

. . . The dilemma facing special educators and all those working in the caring professions and dealing with the adults with learning difficulties is whether they should put their priorities to helping their clients reach the highest possible educational level and high achievement in the labour market or whether they should concentrate more on helping their clients become better integrated into their real social surroundings. (pp. 575-7)

It seems to me to be no surprise that this research and its findings emerged from Budapest, the spiritual and material home of the internationally renowned Conductive Education. This system encourages children with cerebral palsy and related physical disabilities to learn to walk as a key goal in their social integration. Other elements of their educational development are given less priority in this comprehensive preparation for physical mobility and social acceptance. Critics of the system say that it makes walking too important a goal and seeks to 'normalize' children rather than to accept them as they are. Yet Hungary has for long been a poor country with limited specialist resources for disabled people. Quality of life, in a harsh physical context, may well be seen to hang upon mobility skills. Conductive Education is about a holistic curriculum in which educational, physical and social development are all integrated as of equal worth. Bánfalvy's findings are challenging to Western Europeans, used to a competitive materialism. They actually contest the notion that achievement brings happiness. A caring community, in which one feels valued, is more likely to provide a sense of well-being. Of course, both might be ideal, but the striving for achievement against all odds can be a hard personal sacrifice. There are examples of people with learning difficulties whose lives have become more stressful and less fulfilled since they were empowered by professionals to strive for achievement without community networks of support (Dowson, 1997). Really listening to research findings such as these is difficult for caring professionals whose own value systems may be being questioned in the process. After all, in their striving for promotion and professional credibility, have they risked losing community richness and the feeling of being valued for themselves?

(3) Territorial isolation in the institution of the family

In Goffman's (1961) description of 'total institutions', the reference was largely to places like asylums, prisons and hospitals. However, the nuclear family could legitimately be described as a total institution, containing the child during much of its waking hours and fostering routines, rituals and codes of behaviour. It is in this context that disabled children learn how they are valued. Meira Weiss (1997), who is in the Department of Sociology and Social Anthropology at the Hebrew University of Jerusalem, explores the territorial behaviour in the homes of families which contain disabled children.

The examples selected are all of territorial rejection within the home. One baby girl with multiple physical disabilities was not taken home from hospital by her parents and a policeman eventually brought her to their home and made them take responsibility for her. She was kept in the bathroom and it was then no longer used by her siblings until her death at 2 years old, when it was restored to family use. Another family, who were well educated and quite wealthy, rejected their daughter with learning disabilities, who was looked after in a separate area of their home by her own nanny, different from her sibling's nanny. Her mother stressed to the researcher that this was to give her disabled daughter her own territory. In another family, the 12-year-old daughter with Down syndrome was confined largely to the kitchen, where she was expected to serve the domestic needs of the rest of the family. Until her condition was diagnosed at 1 year old, she had been in all the family photos, had a family bedroom upstairs and been with the family in the living room. Now, her bedroom was a bare, small room in the basement next to the laundry. Weiss talked of the child being kept in 'territorial seclusion within the home, in a specially-demarcated area which is considered "non-home" by the parents' (p. 268). This researcher goes on to suggest that:

> The fact that similar forms of territorial rejection were found amongst religious and secular Arab and Jewish families occupying different economic positions, contradicts much of the literature which attributes parents' behaviour to their national or ethnic affiliation. Indeed, the fact that the common pattern of behaviour was observed to cut across various sociodemographic boundaries attests to its deep-rooted psychological causes. (pp. 268-9)

These observations are interesting because they challenge the notion that adults who feel threatened and dislocated within their cultural context will necessarily transfer their fears and anxieties into a protective stance towards the most vulnerable members of their family group. Hostility, prejudice and exploitation towards your own child is a reality which it is difficult for most of us to confront, as the public denial of much physical and sexual abuse of children by parents illustrates. Weiss suggests that the caring professions need to be very cautious in equating the acceptance of a disabled child into the family home as an indication of unconditional love. It may offer a small version of the most oppressive form of institutional confinement, 'reproducing within it the ghetto (jail, institution, servants' corner) designed for the deformed in the past and often also in the present' (p. 269). In a current climate where 'care in the community' usually means that the family are expected to cope, it is important to reflect that caring communities require extensive support networks and friendly neighbours if they are to flourish. As Schwartz (1997) reflected, reliance upon the traditional care-givers can be a sterile option: we all need to be caring and to enjoy the caring experience.

Conclusion: What Can Support a Culture of Caring?

There have been some surprising views explored in this chapter. Perhaps the central one is that of recognizing the value of simple communities and what they can offer to those who are vulnerable. As we approach the millennium, the major publicity is focused upon technological advances, market competitors, global power struggles and potential for growth. It is a world which favours the strong and the clever, the bold and the brave. This can leave behind those who drain national economies, who live on the margins, whose needs can become invisible. In a culture of competitive individualism there have to be losers and their fate is to become passive dependants.

However, the millennium is an opportunity to re-evaluate the way we live in the most advanced societies. In America and Britain there has now developed a cult of 'down-shifting', in which those who have achieved much but feel their quality of life is impoverished in the process are taking risks by opting out into a more simple way of life. We ignore the needs of the marginalized at our peril. Unless inner-city blight is addressed, youth crime will continue to increase. We are coming to realize that the 'care in the community' ideology does not work unless accompanied by a culture of caring. In order to foster such a culture, we in the Northern hemisphere would do well to emulate other societies which place more value on the collective rather than the individual and in which simple ways of life are still able to sustain support systems.

SEVEN

Empowerment and Colonialism: Letting Go

Introduction

The end of the twentieth century is an appropriate time to reflect upon the need to let go of an imperialist past history for a country like Britain which once ruled so much of the world and for whom the beginning of this century was a triumph of colonial power. The passing of Hong Kong from British to Chinese rule on 1 July 1997 marked the death throes of Empire for a once powerful country which may no longer see itself as 'Great' in influence and status. Colonialism, whether benign or oppressive, has meant one group of people having power over another group or groups with the justification that they needed care, protection, guidance and enlightenment. It was one group imposing their way of perceiving the world onto another group, who may perceive it differently from their subordinate position. Whether it be men ruling women, whites ruling blacks, non-disabled ruling disabled or adults ruling children, the tensions between unequal powers and competing needs are felt the same. This is why it is valuable to reflect upon colonialism if we are to develop a fuller understanding of what empowering people with disabilities really means for them and for society in general.

In this chapter, I shall begin by linking the history of the Women's Movement worldwide to the current emancipation of disabled people worldwide. One was a feature of the early 1900s and the other a development of the late 1900s. It seems to me to be important to avoid separating out the needs and expectations of disabled people from those of the population at large. If we reflect upon the way in which women were treated within the last hundred years, we can look ahead to a time when the way in which disabled people are treated will be considered equally unjust and unreasonable.

I shall then go on to define the term 'empowerment' as it is used by professionals who work with disabled people. The self-advocacy movement will be explored in relation to the concept of 'letting go' of power, status and control. The benign and oppressive elements of both colonialism and empowerment will be evaluated as they relate to all minority groups and to disabled people in particular.

The relationship between academics of disability studies and disabled people themselves (including the disabled academics working alongside non-disabled colleagues) can sometimes be tense. Whilst there has developed a recent methodology named 'emancipatory' research, it is difficult to assess the extent to which this has influenced research practice in general. Possible future initiatives are exciting in theory but may be impeded in practice. I shall reflect upon the status, influence and conflicts within disability research and the ways in which this area can be empowering in its procedures.

The issue of empowerment and popular culture is addressed, as it indicates how community values are rarely changed by academic research but by powerful media imagery. The capacity for popular culture to influence stereotypes and so foster empowering representations is explored.

The value and limitations of empowerment are then considered, as it relates to people with learning disabilities. There can be conflicting interests, with parents seeking clear labels for their children, professionals each claiming their own separate expertise and campaigning groups of disabled advocates resisting any attempts at categorization or diagnosis in their adherence to the social model of disability.

The final section of this chapter deals with the pain of letting go. Just as most parents feel pain as well as joy in the letting go of their children into adulthood and independence, so the process of empowerment can be fraught. The following chapter then moves into three case studies of educators who have empowered their students or clients and done so with visionary care.

Emancipation and Change

Looking back in history can be a most valuable way of evaluating our progress, the perennial patterns of human behaviour and the repetition of mistakes and power struggles. In any fight for human rights and freedom, there are times when the effort required can appear overwhelming and it is all too easy to give up and become apathetic and resigned to the status quo. That is why it is important to look back to other struggles for equality and to see that what seemed impossible at the time eventually changed beyond many individuals' wildest dreams. The end of the twentieth century has seen a period of history when a country like South Africa has emerged from a long age of social injustice to a level of emancipation for black people which they could never have anticipated only a few years ago. Mandela himself is perhaps one of the most extraordinary individual symbols of hope in the human spirit. It is this hope which can be sustained in groups currently experiencing social oppression when they observe and reflect upon the ways in which human rights have been fought for and won.

If we return to the beginning of the twentieth century, texts like *The Modern Woman's Rights Movement* (Schirmacher, 1912) indicate powerfully that the suffrage movement was fighting for the right to vote by using political tactics which reflect the prejudices of the period. American women were seen to be at the forefront of the inter-national suffrage movement and were outraged that they were seen as inferior to any kind of men. Schirmacher says that:

This was strikingly impressed upon the women of the United States in 1870. At that time the negroes, who had been emancipated in 1863, were given political rights throughout the Union by the addition of the Fifteenth Amendment to the Federal Constitution. The American woman felt very keenly that in the eyes of their legislators a member of an inferior race, IF ONLY A MAN, should be ranked superior to any woman, be she ever so highly educated; and they expressed their indignation in a picture portraying the American woman and her political associates. This represented the Indian, the idiot, the lunatic, the criminal, — AND WOMAN. In the United States they are all without political rights. (p. 9)

This reflection of perspectives in the early 1900s is useful to us now for we continue to make invidious comparisons whilst concurrently protesting about unequal rights. It has not been uncommon during the 1970s and 1980s for physically disabled people to dissociate themselves from people with learning difficulties or mental health problems. 'You think I am stupid because I cannot speak' was the common retort. This implied a clear hierarchy of disabilities, whereby those with physical and sensory disabilities but without additional learning difficulties were placing themselves as superior to other kinds of disabled people. These are surely perennial tensions which reflect the fragility of the human ego and the inevitability of conflict from within any disparate group, including those who perceive themselves as an oppressed minority.

Situations which seemed hopeless can become hopeful. Schirmacher (1912) reminds us that women in the early 1900s had cause to feel disempowered to an extent which many women in the world no longer experience.

Woman is free and is regarded as a human being only in a very small part of the civilized world. Even in these places we see daily tenacious survivals of the old barbarity and tyranny. Hence it is not true that woman is the 'weaker', the 'protected', the 'loved' and the 'revered' sex. In most cases she is the overworked, exploited, and (even when living in luxury) the oppressed sex. These circumstances dwarf woman's humanity, and limit the development of her individuality, her freedom and her responsibility. These conditions are opposed by the woman's rights movement. The movement hopes to secure the happiness of woman, of man, of the child, and of the world by establishing the equal rights of the sexes. These rights are based on the recognition of equality of merit; they provide for responsibility of action. Most men do not understand this ideal. They oppose it with unconscious egotism. (p. 264)

Much of what Schirmacher (1912) said in relation to the woman's rights movement of the beginning of this century could be said of the disability rights movement in the last quarter of the century. The 'unconscious egotism' of non-disabled people acts as a barrier to true empathy.

In Britain in the late 1990s we have a far higher proportion of women Members of Parliament than ever in the past. Women are to be found among judges, top business executives and in senior posts in every profession. Whilst this does not counter-affect the continued oppression of women in many areas of the world, including the most highly developed countries, it does offer hope that opportunities have opened up and attitudes have changed. It also gives hope to other oppressed groups that change is possible and cultural climates are not fixed.

Empowerment and Letting Go

The issue of control and power between unequal groups in society has long been a source of contention. As Schirmacher said in reference to women, they were often oppressed and denied choice or control over their lives on the grounds that they were weak, needed protection and were unable to cope with difficult, worldly decisions. This maxim has for long been applied to disabled people, particularly to those with learning disabilities. Their childlike social status has denied them decision-making and left them vulnerable to professional exploitation and abuse. Recent research by Corbett, Cottis and Morris (1996) indicates that sexual abuse by staff who were in positions of power over people with learning disabilities has become an issue which professional bodies can no longer avoid confronting. Dowson (1997) refers to the 'pathological culture' (p. 105) of some health, social and education services where power has become abusive and subversive.

Perhaps the first form of 'letting go' necessary in any move towards the taking of power for oneself is that of recognizing that those with ownership of power are not without weaknesses and personal agendas. One of the dilemmas is that systems create their own momentum to such an extent that they generate patterns of behaviour which can become difficult to challenge. Just because something is constructed into a system does not make it good. The system is no more than the amalgamation of ideas of the people who constructed it and, even then, it may be something very different from what was originally intended.

The large asylums which were built to house people with labels of 'lunatic' or 'idiot' were originally intended to be places of sanctuary and protection from the world beyond. They became dreaded forms of social control, the total institutions which destroyed identity and initiative. However, it was not their original design which was evil but the way in which segregated systems generated their own substrata of intimidation and oppression. Education may be seen by the general public as having a benign social role, but not only do many scholars see schooling as a subversive activity, there is also frightening evidence from history that the curriculum can be used as an agent of prejudice. In her extraordinary account of the national curriculum in Nazi Germany of the 1930s, Erika Mann (1939) demonstrates that in every subject area facts were distorted to foster prejudice and hatred of the Jewish people. A whole education system was corrupted and a generation taught to mistrust and fear signs of racial difference. In a situation where power relations were so clearly unequal, it is not surprising that many teachers colluded in this painful process.

One of the important lessons which such an example from our recent history can teach us is that evil policies can become so deeply embedded in the status quo that they colonize the mindset of national agendas. We need to be ever vigilant of this potential for destructive influences. Part of all of our empowerment must be a 'letting go' of what has recently been referred to as 'the nanny state' and a conscious determination to make our own decisions on what our values tell us is right. Conversely, if people with learning disabilities are to feel really empowered, their way of seeing the world they live in and how they experience their lives needs to be respected. This can be very difficult for professionals who are so practised in assessing, judging and defining others. To lay aside your own value judgements and listen with respect to those of people who may live completely different lives from your own is the kind of challenge which many professional educators find almost impossible. It is often difficult enough for them to accept that some people prefer reading the *Sun* to the *Guardian*! Yet, unless we lay aside our egos, our judgements and our professional responses, we are unlikely empowerers. If empowerment equates with emancipation, this has to involve a release from captivity. Nowhere perhaps have disabled people become more captured than in their victim role as research subjects. Here they are used by researchers as data which reflect their powerless status. Even when the researchers see themselves as on the side of disabled people, this does not mean that the research process will necessarily be liberating or lead to any tangible form of progression for the subjects concerned.

Disability Studies and Emancipatory Research

In recent years within British universities departments of Disability Studies have been established, following on from the flourishing departments already well established throughout North America. A new approach to research methodology has emerged from some of these departments which has been termed 'emancipatory research' (Oliver, 1992). This research attempts to confront the inequities within power struggles and to politicize the nature of research on disability so that it places the emancipation of disabled people from their social oppression at its very heart. Not all academics in this field support such an approach. Bury (1996) is sceptical as to its value, suggesting that disabled people are not always the most appropriate researchers and that the research process of itself is not inherently alienating.

It seems important to me that we do not assume that all academics remain in ivory tower seclusion and never risk themselves in bold research adventures. One of the pioneers of emancipatory research who really did (physically and emotionally) release disabled people from captivity was Burton Blatt, Director of Special Education and Rehabilitation at Syracuse University, New York State. In the mid-1960s he and fellow researchers took hidden cameras and notebooks into large and bleak institutions for people with learning disabilities and emerged later to produce *Christmas in Purgatory*, a photographic essay which was to change practice across several states of America. He said:

> The first edition of this book was published in August, 1966, and was distributed without charge under the auspices of a group of parents and friends of the mentally retarded. These thousand copies were sent to prominent legislators, commissioners of mental health, university professors, and leaders in the parent movement in mental retardation. . . . The purpose of this book is to present our findings in the hope that they will inspire constructive action among those in responsible positions. We cannot permit ourselves thoughts of immediate radical reform as a result of our efforts. We can only hope for increased public interest. (Blatt and Kaplan, 1974, p. iii)

The powerful combination of black and white photographs of people in degradation and indignity with detailed descriptive prose was a force for change. For people unable to speak for themselves, it was truly emancipatory. Recent television programmes alerting the public to ill-treatment of vulnerable people in various parts of the world are serving a similar role. It is about the journalistic strength of research which is political and angry.

Peters (1995) calls for the evolution of a disability consciousness through confrontations with existing paradigms. She insists that:

> The capability for change ultimately rests with the authentic voices of people with disabilities. As Joshua Malinga (Secretary General of Disabled Persons International) said during his speech to Zimbabwean SEN professionals in response to the question, 'Why haven't attitudes changed in 2,000 years?': 'Nothing changes until those who feel the pain decide, "Enough is enough!" . . . the field of SEN will succeed in addressing these issues to the extent that it opens its doors to the ideas, leadership and critical analyses of the traditionally marginalised people it has sought to serve: those with disabilities.' (p. 73)

This call for a more empowering professional response is echoing through the halls of academe and has alerted researchers in the special educational needs (SEN) area to be politically correct in the words they use, the proposals they write, the research tools they select, the team which conducts that research project and the way it is finally presented in the public domain. However, we need to be careful to recognize the restricted world in which we operate as academics. We communicate with a small audience. Our influence on attitudes is slight, in the broad scheme of things. It is in the area of popular culture that attitudes and ideas can be most powerfully transformative.

Empowerment and Popular Culture

I feel that any minority group can know for certain that they are seen as an integral element of popular culture once they are represented in television soap operas. Trivial as such programmes may appear to intellectuals, they are important indicators of how the majority feel and think. If minority groups see themselves reflected in the media in popular entertainment rather than as the subjects of heavy documentaries, they know they have arrived. They are visible and real, not just the objects of pity or ridicule.

An interesting current example of this is the soap, *EastEnders*, which has an enormous popular audience in Britain. Two of the characters, in this portrayal of East London life, are young gay men who live together as a couple. Their soap characters completely break the stereotypical media image of limp-wristed, very effeminate, high-camp comics. They are working-class young men, shown in their relationship with siblings, parents, friends and colleagues. They are an integral part of the community and not separate from it. For this very reason, the issues they raise (e.g. 'queer-bashing' — one gets beaten up and a brick is thrown through their window) are powerfully presented. It is not outsiders or the marginalized who are being attacked and persecuted. It is people *inside* the community. This makes for a far more empowering presentation than if they were shown as peripheral figures, shadows without substance and therefore of no general concern.

Disability, as an issue of interest, has to come in from the margins. Whilst some advocates of disability culture foster its ghetto status as a source of cultural cohesion and sub-group resistance, this disempowers it. A marginalized culture speaks to the margins: the mainstream can remain unaware and resolutely complacent. The effective confrontation of prejudice can demand 'in your face' action. This is why the margins need to move into the mainstream, shattering complacent calm in the process.

There are two interesting examples of recent novels which deal with disability and challenge prejudice and narrow stereotypes. One is written by a disabled woman who is in a wheelchair as a result of an accident in adult life. The other is from a non-disabled man whose 'disability' for some years was heroin addiction. Lois Keith (1997) writes of a teenage girl's experience of becoming disabled through a viral infection which leaves her in a wheelchair. She then finds that her comprehensive school is reluctant to take her back as a member of its community as she presents them with physical challenges. This leads the lively heroine of Keith's novel to take assertive action. She mounts a campaign based on the motto 'Use Your Imagination' to confront inflexible professional attitudes. This is a teenage novel written for a teenage market and, as such, a potential tool for fostering empowerment in presenting a strong, forceful heroine who is not prepared to be a recipient of charity but who wants equity on her terms.

Irvine Welsh writes stories of the drug culture in its many dimensions. In this respect, he is a symbol of late twentieth-century degeneracy for some and a role model of acid-head consciousness for others. Either way, his influence as a very successful popular author is considerable. In one of his novellas from *Ecstasy* (1996) he introduces a young woman who was born disabled through her mother taking a drug to alleviate nausea in pregnancy. The heroine has no arms and uses hand flaps on her shoulders. Welsh presents her as an angry, revengeful woman, determined to pursue the businessman who was responsible for marketing the drug despite scientific tests warning him against the ethicality of this. It is fierce, political polemic at one level, but the author also makes his heroine admirable and humane. She is tough, unsentimental and no object of pity. With the support of a non-disabled young man who loves her, she tracks down the businessman and takes her revenge. He is tied to a table in a locked garage and she takes great relish in cutting off *his* arms with a chain-saw. Yes, it is horrible! It is also a total break with the sentimental stereotype of the poor disabled girl needing help. She gets her revenge and empowers herself. It is a late twentieth-century image of capitalism, consumerism and greed creating an angry under-class and disability is its epicentre. Not cosy, but it is right there in the mainstream of anarchic youth culture. So often disabled young people are seen to move from childhood to adulthood, without an adolescent rebellion. Here a disabled young woman is an integral part of the drug culture, abused herself by capitalist drug manufacture, and as violent and anti-establishment as her non-disabled companions.

The Value and Limitations of Empowerment

Two integral elements of effective empowerment are inclusion and communication. What I mean by inclusion, in this instance, is the active seeking out of the views and feelings of disabled people themselves in any research, interventions or treatments. In a recent book called *Seen and Heard* (Ward, 1997), strategies are explored for involving disabled children and young people in research and development projects. There is a recognition that some children will be unable to speak and may need help to communicate their ideas and that others will need support when the process of revealing information is sensitive and potentially painful for them. It is a breakthrough in the world of disability research that the views of children are sought out and listened to as part of an entitlement policy.

Professionals are not immune to the need to give the kind of support which really empowers rather than merely saying it does. Recent work by psychiatrists and psychologists has enabled people with learning disabilities to cope more effectively than before with the ordeal of being arrested by the police and going to court, through very helpful, visually presented texts (Hollins *et al.*, 1996). The pictures can be used with their social worker or key care manager, to talk them through what is a frightening procedure. This is a most powerful way of both giving them appropriate assistance and treating them as responsible adults. Empowerment is not about 'dropping people in it' and letting them sink or swim. Such an attitude has surely given a bad name to empowerment. It is about recognizing what vulnerable people within the community may need and helping them to develop the skills and experience which give them confidence and strength. It has to involve some risk and some loss of authority.

The value of empowerment is that it can make excluded people feel that they can communicate their ideas and participate in debates beyond the narrow frontiers of a segregated society. The limits are that it may make them believe that they will have access to positions of power which are still denied to them, so compounding their disappointment with the pain of unmet expectations. A recent issue raised in the Mencap journal *Viewpoint* (July 1997) illustrates this clearly. Swindon People First wanted to remain a user-led organization in which people with learning disabilities were trustees, when it applied to the Charity Commission to become a registered charity. The group were told that people with learning disabilities were not appropriate to be trustees, even though London People First had already won this battle in 1992 and the group at Swindon People First were apparently coping effectively. If empowerment is about confidence-building, this inflexible bureaucracy is profoundly disempowering in its incapacity to trust, take risks or accept new ways of working. The need to let go of the old and embrace the new is palpable: so is the fear of failure.

It is important also to recognize that for all the rejection of biological and medical models of disability as outdated, unhelpful and unreasonable, by disabled activists like Shakespeare (1997), there are still parent groups who actively seek biological and medical labels, as journals like *NEWS: Research Trust for Metabolic Diseases in Children* illustrate. Such journals serve to inform parents and to clarify understanding (e.g. 'Recent advances in our understanding of Canavan Disease', Bennett, 1994). Many parents whose children have unusual syndromes or who know they are genetically vulnerable to specific disabilities want to have access to detailed diagnosis and treatment stories from other parents: this is their empowerment. If we are to respect the empowerment of disabled people, should we not also respect the empowerment of parents who want knowledge and communication networks?

The Pain of Letting Go

Dowson (1997) suggests that history tells us that people rarely give up power: they either find it too costly to hang on to or they have it taken away from them. Perhaps both of these experiences are affecting professional power at the end of twentieth-century Britain. Old professional hierarchies and status are eroded within the privatization of public sector services. Doctors, social workers and teachers are being directed by new management strategies designed for market-effectiveness, cost-cutting and consumer-friendliness. Their former role as experts is threatened. The fragility of expertise is evident and they, too, can be seen to be disempowered. This applies to professors in the new higher education, where market ideologies have located learning in many contexts other than traditional universities (Pratt, 1997). It also applies to adult educators in colleges where they are committed to empowering unemployed adults when they themselves are struggling with the insecurity of short-term contracts and uncertain goals (Walker, 1997). Disempowered staff working with disempowered people can be seen as a common feature of the recent developments in the public sector and a familiar cause of disenchantment and despair.

Are there ways in which the relinquishing of power is not painful? Perhaps one of the first essentials is not to care too much about having authority in the first place. The three case studies which make up the concluding chapter of this book are of staff who know what they want to do in their practice but who are not apparently concerned to compromise for ambition. They are not in very powerful institutional roles, in the conventional sense, yet are tremendously powerful in their impact upon the daily lives of the disabled people they work alongside. Their power resides in their vision. They see ways in which the quality of life can be made richer for the people they work with and they use their respective creative gifts to foster this development. The rewards are in the growth of confidence in relatively powerless people. In each example, this visionary work is difficult to measure as a series of competencies. Yet, in each case, they have proved to be pioneers in responding to market trends.

EIGHT

Care with Vision:
A New Role for Professionals

Introduction

In order to illustrate what I feel is truly empowering in professional behaviour towards people with disabilities, I have decided to end the book with three specific examples of what I consider to be care which is given with imagination, sensitivity and respect: care with vision. Like Schwartz (1997), I want to take examples from my own experience of community. In so doing, I can present the level of detailed analysis which helps towards an evaluation of what empowerment can really mean in daily practice.

In this concluding chapter, I shall pull together some of the key threads of my debates within the overall text. These are the following:

(1) the significance of E-mapping, or entitlement to services, for different groups and individuals and what this means for quality of life;
(2) the legacy of routine and ritual in professional service delivery and the implications of this for receptivity to change and flexibility;
(3) the value of simplicity in community living and the limitations of an achievement-dominated culture;
(4) the importance of perceiving schools as just part of community provision, to be linked with other systems and services to form a coherent whole;
(5) the need to listen to visionary thinkers, whose ideas may be ahead of their time, for they may be forecasting the pathways of the future.

This chapter will look at collaboration beyond the disability community into the institutional community and into the community at large. It will examine the work of three pioneering educators whose commitment to the valuing of disabled people as individuals with dignity has led them to think beyond immediate needs into planning for a more responsive service. All three practitioners are working in Britain, although their approaches are also to be found in America and elsewhere. I have selected them because they are part of my community and the culture I understand. I feel able to discuss their work from having observed it in operation rather than from second-hand accounts.

The first example began her pioneering work from a segregated special school setting. The second example is within a multimedia community arts project, now incorporated into the life of a university. The third example is working within the community, in disability arts, developing systems which will enhance the care delivery offered by social services. All three are to some extent operating 'from the edge', in presenting a new and refreshing angle on the area of special provision with which they are connected.

Art Appreciation for Children with Learning Disabilities

Chitra Aloysius has worked for many years in the special school sector as a teacher of children with complex and multiple disabilities. Many teachers would see this as the most segregated form of schooling and the least inclusive in terms of its limited range of curricula and clientele. For many special educators, it is also seen as the centre of expertise in which individual pupils are following tailor-made programmes designed to respond to their specific difficulties. There is usually an emphasis upon basic skills, self-help and communication skills in order to address the evident difficulties of the pupils. The programme often consists of mixtures of the following, according to need: literacy- and numeracy-based activities; communication activities initiated by speech therapists; mobility activities initiated by physiotherapists; daily living skills activities to prepare young people to cook, clean, shop and budget for their lives in the community. If one were to assess where these elements come within a basic hierarchy of needs continuum, it would be at the very lowest level of fundamental learning in a very concrete form.

Art appreciation may be generally seen as a highly abstract concept. It is related to sensibilities and aesthetic awareness. Within British culture, high art is often regarded as something which only the well-educated can appreciate. Part of our cultural divisiveness is that high and low art tends to define class, intelligence and levels of refinement. Whilst intellectuals may support football teams, it is less common to find young gangs of football supporters in art galleries and museums. The public perception is that high art is for 'highbrows'.

When Chitra began her studies on the value of art appreciation for children with moderate learning difficulties in the late 1980s, she was going against the dominant basic skills emphasis prevalent in special schooling at that time. Her Master's degree project to record and evaluate the benefits of art appreciation for children with moderate learning difficulties grew out of her conviction that all children could enjoy and value art at whatever level. She established a lunchtime art club which was quickly well attended as children spread the word that looking at pictures was fun. This was the key to her communication. She made Picasso, Renoir, Monet and many of the 'Great Masters' exciting for these children who were unfamiliar with galleries or paintings. She initiated them into this experience by careful preparation for gallery visits.

> The aims of the art club were to increase the children's sensitivity to their own world and their capacity for enjoyment and to bridge the gap between the past depicted by the artist and the present experienced by the child. (Pearson and Aloysius, 1994, p. 16)

It seems significant to me that this teaching reflects a powerful combination of professional skill, thoughtful planning, courageous vision and active caring. What do I mean by 'active caring'? In my reflection on my own experience of teaching in special schools, I considered the concept of 'careful' teaching, by which I meant a form of interaction with vulnerable learners which gave them respect, dignity and a sense of self-worth (Corbett, 1992). This kind of care is more than just loving the children, in a sentimental and potentially patronizing way. It is about valuing them for themselves and being responsive to their forms of expression. This involves a removal of imposed judgements and value systems which define how and where things *ought* to be done. That is why quality caring is visionary: it breaks boundaries and establishes new ways of seeing.

Chitra is a visionary teacher. Her adherence to art appreciation for children with learning difficulties was regarded with some scepticism by education officers in her authority who felt the teaching of basic skills to be the main priority. She resolutely held on to her vision of the value of art appreciation and had high expectations of the children, such that she anticipated that they would select the art club rather than the playground in their lunch-hour. Through her visionary caring, Chitra moved on to introduce art appreciation to a wide range of children, some of whom had more complex disabilities. Their appreciation of gallery visits was recorded by her:

> Jamie, a child with moderate learning difficulties and behavioural problems who has poor concentration and struggles to write his own name said, 'When I look at paintings it makes me think of other artists and feel like them. I don't just draw. I think how to draw and want to do better, and this makes me happy.' (Pearson and Aloysius, 1994, p. 18)

Because she had familiarized the children with the works they went to view, they were confident enough to offer critical commentary. Being prepared so carefully, they saw the paintings as old friends and the art gallery as a welcoming space. Chitra's vision may have seemed out of place in the small world of segregated special schooling, but in the wider arena of art galleries and museums it proved to be exactly what was being sought and seen as a priority for future development. She went on to work collabora- tively with staff at the British Museum to produce a teaching pack and a book, *The Big Foot: Museums and Children with Learning Difficulties* (Pearson and Aloysius, 1994). This has been used as a model of good practice in Britain and America and initiated more national projects to help high culture become more inclusive. Like all visionary thinkers, she was foreseeing a future development and stepping in where others either feared to tread or lacked the imagination to do so.

This example of teaching which opens out a wider experience to children whose educational diet is usually considerably constrained illustrates the key issues raised in this book:

- *(E-mapping)* What different groups of people are seen to want or need is often restricted by narrow stereotypes of their capabilities and limitations. This is partic- ularly true of those regarded as intellectually deficient. The most aesthetic experiences of art, music, poetry and theatre can be accessible to people of widely different past experiences if they really feel included. Chitra made the galleries and museums inclusive by preparing her pupils and making the strange familiar to them. Their entitlement to these rich cultural experiences was balanced alongside their entitlement to basic skills.

- *(the legacy of routine and ritual)* For teachers like Chitra, to innovate the special curriculum by introducing unusual subject areas and imaginative ways of experiencing ideas is a high-risk activity, often met with a mixture of ridicule, apathy and resistance. The more segregated an institution is, the more likely it is to be governed by routine and ritual. Patterns of behaviour which may be perpetuating outdated and redundant activities are justified on the grounds that 'We've always done it like this'. Inclusive education has not yet involved the wholesale closure of special schooling in Britain or elsewhere. If anything, special schools have become ever more segregated and exclusive as their composition has changed to accommodate children with more profound disabilities. Flexibility and receptivity to change has to include imaginative approaches to the curriculum and the constant challenging of habitual practices.

- *(the value of simplicity in community living)* In an achievement-dominated culture, where competencies are measured and evaluated, 'mastery of skills' and gaining high marks in examinations become markers of success and it is easy to lose sight of core values. By 'core values' I mean the qualities which define us as responsive, alert, caring and fulfilled human beings. In a complicated culture of goal-setting and task-centred competitiveness, it is often *simplicity* which becomes the most difficult goal to achieve. It seems ironic to me that the more complex and stressful societies become (particularly those of Western Europe and North America), the more many people strive to regain simplicity and to enjoy what they see as the simple life where they express core values. Chitra shows that art and artefacts can be enjoyed and understood at a simple as well as a complex level and that valuing beauty, vitality and our humanity is open to us all.

- *(schools as part of their community)* Special schools are highly exclusive and can risk being isolated from their local, let alone their wider, community. As a response to this, past initiatives have involved links with local sports centres, mainstream schools, colleges and parent groups. However, there are many different resources in the community and it can be easy to overlook those which appear to be unrelated to the evident needs of students with learning disabilities. The arts generally are not necessarily important to wide sections of the population but they can be enjoyed by many diverse groups of people. Opera is not just for the rich. There are pensioners and people on benefits who regularly attend in cheap seats. The arts should be for anyone who wants to enjoy them. To ensure that people with learning disabilities can become part of this wider community of music, art, drama and dance is to offer them real inclusion in all aspects of community resources, not just those educational, recreational and social facilities deemed useful. We do not only explore our communities for 'useful' reasons. We often need to have infusions of imaginative insights and playfulness which the arts, in their varied forms, can supply. This imaginative intake is of value to all, at whatever level it is received.

■ *(listening to visionary thinkers)* Teachers like Chitra are a great gift to special education. It seems unlikely that the special school system will dissolve in the immediate future and, therefore, we have to consider its relevance to the beginning of the twenty-first century. It is important for us to acknowledge that, in many areas of the world, it is the establishment of special schools which is the marker of progress, rather than the impetus for inclusive education coming from North America and Western Europe. Whilst special schools remain a facet of schooling at the end of the twentieth century, if they are to be responsive to change they require visionary teachers to ensure their continued adaptability. Within historical terms, the curriculum of British special schools is relatively recent in its evolution and has gradually been broadened to include elements of the National Curriculum alongside basic skills. There is scope for innovation within a values-based ideology. Teachers like Chitra can both introduce exciting new experiences for pupils and give messages to their colleagues and to parents that these children have a capacity to be critical observers of their own culture. They are part of that culture, not excluded from it.

A Multimedia Project in a University

Stuart Olesker had worked in a multimedia scheme at Portsmouth College of Art, Design and Further Education for some years when it became incorporated into the new University of Portsmouth. This meant that the diverse range of students included within the scheme, some of whom had complex learning disabilities, mental health difficulties and physical disabilities, had become university rather than college students. The nature of their course was challenging to a university in that it was essentially a response-centred curriculum and teaching approach, along the lines of that described by the American arts teachers in Chapter 6 (Smith Livdahl, 1995). The students are encouraged to run meetings, direct projects and take control of their group activities. Olesker (1992) said of the scheme as it existed in the early 1990s:

> Prospective students tend to consider the multi-media scheme after eliminating other possibilities. If they do not know what they want, they know what they do not want: not school, not set college syllabus, not residential home, not training scheme, not assessment, not sheltered employment, not activity centre. (p. 77)

In these respects, the scheme was able to offer an alternative further education experience which bridged a range of possibilities, allowed for flexible approaches and was error-permitted learning. Yet it had emerged from what was historically characteristic of further education options in the mid-1980s. Youth Training Schemes were then presented as a major resource for 16-year-olds seeking pre-vocational provision and opportunities for trainees with disabilities and learning difficulties were wide-ranging. As these schemes ended, the further education colleges developed more flexible provision to include diverse learners. The shift to a focus on education rather than training allowed for more flexibility within the curriculum.

With the recent acquisition of university status, the multimedia course is now an element of a broader programme which includes students on 'English and creative studies' courses spending a term within the scheme, to work collaboratively with the wide range of learners to produce completed projects. In this respect, what could be seen as a potentially 'token' form of integration within the exclusive institution of a university has become an inclusive provision in which students learn from each other and share skills in a forum which values co-operative learning. It is significant that the mainstream students who participate are not training to be teachers, social workers, nurses or other health professionals: they are not learning how to be good carers in a professional sense. They are doing degrees in the arts and work with this group to produce final results which will satisfy them as creative artists, directors and performers. When I researched integration schemes in further education over the last fifteen years, they were so often involving students preparing to enter the 'caring' professions. This multimedia project seems to me to be one of the most truly inclusive post-school programmes I have come across.

Having observed Stuart working with groups of students, I would say that his approach fosters community rather than individualistic values. It is not about ego or competitiveness. The students have diverse needs with their main shared experience being lack of confidence and self-esteem. Some want to do drama for itself in order to learn the skills which will take them onto other degree courses, whilst others are using it as a therapy. There is a high level of group empathy and support and a tangible nurturing of each other. What impressed me most was Stuart's capacity to act as a facilitator to learning and not to intervene unless asked to do so by students. One of the group was directing the others in an improvised drama and some were responsible for sound and lighting. The nature of improvised work involved group discussion about possible developments and a sharing of ideas. Everyone's ideas were given equal worth. It would have been all too easy for Stuart, an experienced actor and stage director, to have taken over and, in so doing, ensure that the productions reached the highest level of perfection achievable. He could have imposed his standards on the group and risked inhibiting their initiative. Instead, he holds back whilst they struggle, reconceptualize, make mistakes, go off at a tangent and then find their own collective ways to cope. It is error-permitted learning and the process is clearly as valuable as the end result.

I have come increasingly to feel that the concept of 'good enough' is the key to productive community values. Striving for an elusive personal perfection is frustrating, anxiety-making and ultimately destructive. One of the reasons why teachers like Stuart and Chitra seem so successful in genuinely empowering their students (i.e. giving power away) is that they can embrace 'good enough' with a courageous trust in the capacities of the learners they work with. Chitra knows that those children she shares works of art with will value them on their terms and that, for her, is 'good enough'. That she experiences the paintings at a more complex and profound level (i.e. with expertise) is beside the point. What pleases her can please these learners: she respects their sense of being. Equally, with Stuart, his respect for the students stops him acting as critical teacher but he is there as a critical friend, to provide valuable support but not in charge, gently encouraging experiences at many levels of proficiency.

Within the key issues raised in the book, this example illustrates that:

- *(E-mapping)* Higher education can be accessible as an entitlement at different levels and for different purposes to many learners, not just those who have traditionally attended.
- *(the legacy of routine and ritual)* For this to work effectively, it requires that teachers in universities learn to adapt to different learning styles and to become flexible and responsive to meet changing needs.
- *(the value of simplicity in community living)* Universities are highly complex communities, with systems which can serve to alienate individual growth. The inclusion of new groups calls for a respect for simplicity, in the sense of accepting diversity as a richness, not as a problem.
- *(schools/universities as part of the wider community)* At a period of massive global economic change, universities are becoming just one element in the delivery of mass higher education and, as such, need to be receptive to innovation and potential new client groups.
- *(the need to listen to visionary thinkers)* Those professionals who have moved from one sector to another and whose work takes them into community initiatives are often rich resources for evaluating where needs are unmet and what community priorities may be arising in the near future.

Visionary thinkers are not necessarily 'head in the clouds' and impractical, producing utopian ideas which can never be realizable. Quite to the contrary, they are often ahead of their time but absolutely accurate in assessing potential developments. With each of the visionary thinkers I describe in this concluding chapter, their capacity to plug into community needs is remarkable.

Service Delivery and Disability Arts

The two distinct areas of service delivery and disability arts are aspects of community living for disabled people which may seem to have little in common apart from their joint clientele. Care packages are designed by collaboration between social, health and education service-providers to create individual programmes for disabled people who are living in community care. In Schwartz's (1997) analysis, this kind of collaborative care often lacks the human touch when it is composed entirely of professional help: people paid to care for strangers. Yet it is unrealistic to expect that neighbours are necessarily going to display the community values which contribute so evidently to quality experiences in community living. The challenge is to bring the human touch into service-delivery care packages.

John Ladle is the director of the disability arts project Acting Up, which has been operating in London over the last few years. He describes its work as deliberately rejecting the notion that disabled people have nothing to say in relation to their daily lives. Since 1986 Acting Up has worked as an integrated group of professional performers, trainers, media artists and people with profound learning difficulties expressing a shared creative experience. 'Professional' boundaries are challenged as play becomes a rich learning process for all concerned. The group has made videos with adults with learning disabilities, using sound, colour and their daily lived experiences in varied settings including those of long-stay institutions and homes in the community. Institutions can deny personal identity and disempower people with learning disabilities. Acting Up created 'The Soft Room', which was a safe responsive space within the institution in which physical language and concrete stimulus helped to overcome conventional communication barriers. It offered people relationships on their terms and started from where they were comfortable. My impression, on seeing their work, is that it is empowering of itself in providing positive outlets for self-expression for a group of people usually represented in the media in negative, tragic imagery.

Through the development of multimedia profiling (a computer-based combination of text, sound, picture and video), 'silent, invisible people are being given a voice and a presence' (Ladle, 1995, p. 15). People who often have little verbal communication are supported in producing their own audio-visual diaries of daily life and personal history. These are used to provide accessible and negotiable ways for people with profound disabilities to communicate their needs and wishes, so entering into a properly person-centred care programme. An example of this process in action is the use of specific software which enables people preparing to move into a room of their own for the first time to decide on the placement of furniture and decorations, by moving around images on the screen. This might be as simple as the arrangement of the height of a sink, the position of a chair or the inclusion of a picture on the wall. This level of decision-making may appear rather facile but it does mean that the feelings and views of the person concerned are respected. It also necessitates careful listening on behalf of service-providers which can develop into a rapport of a higher quality than that which exists when services are just provided on behalf of the service-user. Such a process fosters confidence in the service-user to demonstrate choice and to control their own personal space.

The profile which is built up becomes the user's catalogue and complements existing text-based records and review systems. It is helpful for such things as continuity of care, respect for individual differences and practical preferences related to toileting, feeding, lifting and everyday needs. Used as a resource tool beyond the limits of written file notes, multimedia profiling can be truly empowering at both the individual and the collective level. Supported with Lottery funding, Acting Up is now expanding its influence beyond London to foster innovation in using communicative facilities and approaches.

At the level of the individual, it effectively challenges the traditional institutional methods of recording because it is compiled with the service-user who becomes centrally involved in developing their own care package and in selecting the images they prefer to represent them, their needs and preferences. At the level of the collective, it has the potential to change the way that social service-providers have traditionally organized services.

In relation to the key issues raised in this book, John's initiative reflects that:

- *(E-mapping)* Even silent and invisible people are entitled to be heard.
- *(the legacy of routine and ritual)* Established patterns of service delivery ('It has worked well like this for years') can be challenged to include the voices of users,

however difficult it might be to listen to them carefully.

- *(the value of simplicity in community living)* Very simple things, like where pieces of furniture might be placed in a room, can be integral to an individual's sense of personal identity and social worth.
- *(the importance of perceiving disability arts as part of community provision)* Disability arts, a fringe activity, are able to link into major structural provision like service-delivery to facilitate new ways of operating.
- *(the need to listen to visionary thinkers)* Seemingly disparate elements of community provision can learn from each other and creative thinking can be harnessed into pragmatic planning to enhance quality assurance for services.

Conclusion: Collaboration and Community

In this concluding chapter I have offered three examples of what I regard as care with vision. They each relate to different aspects of community and distinctive forms of collaborative ways of working.

Chitra worked within a small community in the segregated special school sector. Yet her wider collaboration was with the world of public arts provision. The complex bureaucratic structures of which art galleries and museums are a part can define what counts as culture and who this culture is for. Earlier in the twentieth century, it is most unlikely that people with learning disabilities would have been regarded as suitable visitors to art galleries and museums. The distinction between high art and low art was very marked and only people of a certain class, background and education would have been seen as those seeking this form of culture. It says much of the force of social change and the opening up of opportunities that the National Gallery and the British Museum sought out the services of a teacher like Chitra in the late 1980s. The time was right to include a wider range of people in these cultural experiences and Chitra had the vision to instigate and guide this process.

In his multimedia project, Stuart ensures that students have the opportunity to be included within a university community which offers stimulus, diversity and intel-lectual challenge. For some of his students, their choice is to remain inside a small community composed predominantly of others with similar needs to themselves. For others, it is to move on into other more inclusive courses and to use the multimedia project as a step towards progression. By using the university television studios, these students have access to resources they might not otherwise have used and their expec-tations of themselves are often raised through being in this kind of environment.

At a period when universities in Britain and other parts of Europe are in the process of redefining their role and adjusting to becoming no longer as exclusive as in the earlier years of this century, the issue of differentiated learning has to be addressed. Whilst this concept is widely accepted in schools as appropriate in relation to mixed-ability groups, it is not yet either understood or accepted in higher education. There is some resistance in British higher education to the inclusion of those learners who are prepared to label themselves as having learning disabilities. Whilst it seems likely that Britain will follow North America in making its undergraduate provision serve as a bridge between further and higher education, this remains a challenge to many higher education lecturers who will need to alter their teaching approaches to make them more accessible at different levels.

For both Chitra and Stuart their commitment is to communal values and to the concept of education for all, to be valued as the sharing of rich experiences without limitations but lacking easy measures of progress. This is against the current closely monitored assessment procedures in education generally. There is a tension between measures of competencies and outcomes-related assessment and this form of learner-centred evaluation which could be seen as peripheral to the economy. They could be challenged on the grounds that their work is impossible to assess by standard means and that it therefore may lack rigour. Yet their expectations are high and are structured by ensuring that preparation and support frameworks are in place so that their learners feel safe enough to take risks. I would not underestimate the quality of background awareness which enables this learning to be meaningful.

John's use of multimedia resources to produce flexible and imaginative filing systems to be used by social and health services epitomizes the current attitudes to empowerment as a process and not a product. It is a rich example of collaborative working: collaboration between client and disability arts staff; collaboration between client and services, using the resources produced through the earlier collaboration. In each instance, the client is central.

These three case studies illustrate a new role for professionals, which recognizes community values. They work variously in micro- or macro-communities: special school, university, disability arts (micro); high cultural venues, post-school opportunities, and service-delivery options (macro). They demonstrate that education is not just what happens in institutions. It is about how we interrelate and about the quality of our responsiveness. In my mind, all three of these professionals display the following characteristics: imagination; a vision of what they want to achieve; receptivity to change; a valuing of those whose needs they serve; high expectations of the quality of life they wish for these people. They are all collaborators, working with others in various roles to create improved communication and greater access to quality community services. In each case, they may be seen as mavericks or idealists, unafraid to venture into uncharted waters. They take risks because they are committed to communal rather than individualistic values.

In the Britain of the last fifteen years, it has become increasingly unfashionable to prize community above self. This attitude may suit the enterprise culture but it can only be damaging to the sense of connectedness and collective awareness which gives worth to *all* regardless of their economic capital. The Disability Rights Movement has challenged professional expertise as a disempowering force which alienates them and sees them as 'other'. It does not have to be like this for the future. There are professionals around like Chitra, Stuart and John whose communal values respect difference and who show no reluctance to let go of power. They then become valuable collabo rators, good listeners and reliable allies. There is still a role for expertise, in that having unequal levels of knowledge and experience is an inevitable part of community life. Yet the expert can learn to share. This means letting go and trusting that other ways of seeing the world can be considered without the imposition of a pathologizing analysis. The combination of care and vision is a potent mix. It has the potential to ensure that the views of disabled people are heard, valued and acted upon in twenty-first-century policies and practices. We may then be asking 'Whose needs are special?' if notions of need become subsumed in an adherence to communal values of shared care and collaboration.

Each of the examples in this chapter demonstrates the value and risk of *widening participation*, the very words used by Sir Ron Dearing in a radio interview on 23 July 1997, when his report on higher education into the twenty-first century was published. Participation in all aspects of cultural experience, in higher education and in the control of social care services is no longer for the privileged few but for the many. This creates complications and contradictions. If it becomes for all, then is it devalued and diminished as an experience? Some will argue that children with learning disabilities will get very little out of looking at great works of art or artefacts and that it is not worth the trouble of encouraging their participation. There are already many critics of the expansion of higher education who argue that letting so many people participate means that a degree has low currency and their inclusion changes the cultural context of universities. The increased participation of service-users in deciding the detail of their care provision is regarded as contentious in a climate where limited resources are fought for. Widening participation does not mean creating a fair or just society. It may, however, mean the encouragement of a communal frame of reference within the public sector which places participation as a high priority in determining quality of life. To return to the quote which prefaced this book, Helen Keller (1913) saw that residential schools for blind children were part of the history of special school policy-making, response-driven rather than based upon understanding of long-term needs. She saw participation as being of fundamental value to the lifetime learning and sharing of individuals with disabilities and those who learnt, worked and lived alongside them. A visionary at the beginning of this century, she serves as a model for future growth. Widening participation includes the sharing of skills and rich learning experiences by the transfer of ideas between different countries. Sometimes it is the affluent countries which share resources with the poor. Other times, complex, busy societies can learn how to work towards simplicity: to participate in the art of *being*.

Bibliography

Advisory Council for Education (ACE) (1996) 'Inclusion is a human right, say campaigners', *ACE Bulletin*, 69, February, 5.

Bánfalvy, C. (1996) 'The paradox of the quality of life of adults with learning difficulties', *Disability and Society*, 11, 4, 569–78.

Barber, M. (1993) 'Raising standards in deprived urban areas' in National Commission on Education, *Briefings*. London: Heinemann.

Barnes, D. (1995) *The Making of a Social Disease: Tuberculosis in Nineteenth Century France*. Berkeley: University of California.

Bar-On, Arnon (1997) 'Criminalising survival: images and reality of street children', *Journal of Social Policy*, 26, 1, 63–78.

Barton, L. (1996) 'Sociological perspectives', paper given at Royal Society of Medicine conference on 'Physical Disability: Meeting the Challenges', 6–7 November 1996.

Bennett, M. (1994) 'Recent advances in our understanding of Canavan Disease', *NEWS: Research Trust for Metabolic Diseases in Children*, 4, 7, 6–7.

Blatt, B. and Kaplan, F. (1974) *Christmas in Purgatory*. Syracuse, NY: Human Policy Press.

Bowers, T. (1996) 'Is special needs spending out of control?', *Managing Schools Today*, 5, 33–6.

Briggs, C. (1996) 'The politics of discursive authority in research on "The invention of tradition"', *Cultural Anthropology*, 11, 4, 435–69.

Burt, C. (1992) *Mental and Scholastic Tests*. London: P. S. King and Son, Ltd.

Bury, M. (1996) 'Defining and researching disability: challenges and responses' in Barnes, C. and Mercer, G. (eds) *Exploring the Divide: Illness and Disability*. Leeds: The Disability Press.

Butzer, H. (1995) 'Back to the old ways? The universities have atrophied to providers of services', *European Education*, 26, 4, 6–11.

Campbell, R. (1922) *The Amazing Schoolmaster*. London: Cecil Palmer.

Casson, W. and Whiteley, C. (1903) *The Education Act, 1902*. London: Knight & Co.

Churchill, J., Brown, H., Graft, A. and Horrocks, C. (eds) (1997) *There Are No Easy Answers*. Chesterfield, Nottingham: Arc and Napsal.

Clark, C., Dyson, A., Millward, A. J. and Skidmore, D. (1997) *New Directions in Special Needs: Innovations in Mainstream Schools*. London: Cassell.

Colquhoun, P. (1971; 1st edn 1806) *A New and Appropriate System of Education for the Labouring People*. Shannon: Irish University Press.

Corbett, A., Cottis, T. and Morris, S. (1996) *Witnessing, Nurturing, Protesting: Therapeutic Responses to Sexual Abuse of People with Learning Disabilities*. London: David Fulton.

Corbett, J. (1992) 'Careful teaching: researching a special career', *British Educational Research Journal*, 18, 3, 235–43.

Corbett, J. and McGinty, J. (1996) 'Responding to consumer needs: working towards a quality service' in Wolfendale, S. and Corbett, J. (eds) *Opening Doors: Learning Support in Higher Education*. London: Cassell.

Corbett, J. and Ralph, S. (1994) 'Empowering adults: the changing imagery of charity advertising', *Australian Disability Review*, 94, 1, 5–14.

Crawford, M. (1992) *The Literacy Challenge: Struggle for Early Intervention for Literacy and Learning for Australian Children*. Canberra: Australian Government Publishers.

Crowhurst, G. (1996) 'Fooling the scientists was just show business', *Community Living*, 10, 2, 12.

D.C.L. (1878) *The Education Craze and its Results: School Boards, Their extravagance and inefficiency*. London: Harrison and Sons.

Dowson, S. (1997) 'Empowerment within services: a comfortable delusion' in Ramcharan, P., Roberts, G., Grant, G. and Barland, J. (eds) *Empowerment in Everyday Life*. London: Jessica Kingsley Publishers.

Erevelles, N. (1996) 'Disability and the dialectics of difference', *Disability and Society*, 11, 4, 519–37.

Ford, D. (1996) *Reversing Underachievement Among Gifted Black Students*. New York: Teachers College Press.

French, S. and Swain, J. (1997) *From a Different Viewpoint: The Lives and Experiences of Visually Impaired People*. New York and London: Jessica Kingsley.

Garland Thomson, R. (1997) *Extraordinary Bodies: Figuring Physical Disability in American Culture and Literature*. New York: Columbia University Press.

Garrett, J. (1928) *Mass Education in England*. London: Ed. J. Burrow and Co. Ltd.

Gaspari, R. (1995) 'We need a ghetto', *The Disability Rag and Resource*, May/June 1995, 16–20.

Giordano, G. (1996) *Literacy: Programs for Adults with Developmental Disabilities*. San Diego: Singular Publishing Group, Inc.

Goffman, E. (1961) *Asylums*. Harmondsworth: Penguin Books.

Gross, J. (1996) 'The weight of evidence: parental advocacy and resource allocation to children with statements of SEN', *Support for Learning*, 11, 3–8.

Hastie, R. (1997) *Disabled Children in a Society at War: A Casebook from Bosnia*. Oxford: Oxfam UK and Ireland.

Hellier, C. (1996) 'Reading for Sure: accessing text through diacritical marks', *Support for Learning*, 11, 3, 130–4.

Higg, J. and Mittler, P. (eds) (1980) *Advances in Mental Handicap Research*, Vol. 1. Chichester: John Wiley and Sons.

Hill, D. and Cole, M. (1997) 'Introduction', in Cole, M., Hill, D. and Shan, S. (eds) *Promoting Equality in Primary Schools*. London: Cassell.

Hollins, S., Clare, I. and Murphy, G. (1996) *You're Under Arrest*. London: Gaskell Press/St George's Hospital Medical School.

Hornby, G., Atkinson, M. and Howard, J. (1997) *Controversial Issues in Special Education*. London: David Fulton.

Howe, K. and Miramontes, O. (1992) *The Ethics of Special Education*. New York: Teachers College Press.

Jasperwherrett, G. (1977) *The Miracle of the Empty Beds: A History of Tuberculosis in Canada*. Toronto and Buffalo: University of Toronto Press.

Keith, L. (1997) *A Different Life*. London: The Women's Press.

Keller, H. (1913) *Out of the Dark*. London: Hodder and Stoughton.

Kendall, F. (1996) *Diversity in the Classroom*. New York: Teachers College Press.

Kerzner Lipsky, D. and Gartner, A. (1997) *Inclusion and School Reform*. Baltimore: Paul Brookes Publishing Co.

Kirk, S. and Orville Johnson, G. (1954) *Educating the Retarded Child*. Lonela: George G. Harrap.

Ladle, J. in Crowhurst, G. (1995) 'Giving "invisible" people voices', *Community Living*, October 1995, 14–15.

Lane, H. (1915) 'The faults and misdemeanours of children' in *Report of the Conference on New Ideals in Education* held at Stratford-on-Avon, 14–21 August 1915, pp. 38–52.

Lawton, D. (1997) 'Values and education: a curriculum for the 21st century', paper in conference on 'Values and the Curriculum', Institute of Education, University of London, 10–11 April 1997.

Li Xiaopeng (1997) 'Can those children become "Good Cats"?: dilemmas in the curriculum reform in the schools in Beijing, China', paper in conference on 'Values and the Curriculum', Institute of Education, University of London, 10–11 April 1997.

McCreesh, J. and Maher, A. (1974) *Remedial Education: Objectives and Techniques*. London: Ward Lock Educational.

Mann, F. (1939) *School for Barbarians: Education under the Nazis*. London: Lindsay Drummond Ltd.

Matsaniotis, N. (1996) 'AIDS and children' in Nakou, S. and Pantelakis, S. (eds) *The Child in the World of Tomorrow*. Oxford: Pergamon.

Mazurek, K. and Winzer, M. (eds) (1994) *Comparative Studies in Special Education*. Washington: Gallandet University Press.

Miles, M. (1996) 'Community, individual or information development? Dilemmas of concept and culture in South Asian disability planning', *Disability and Society*, 11, 4, 485–500.

Millard, F. J. C. (1996) 'The rising incidence of tuberculosis', *Journal of the Royal Society of Medicine*, 89, 9, 497–500.

Mittler, P. (1993) 'Childhood disability: a global challenge' in Miller, P., Brouillette, R. and Harris, D. (eds) *Special Needs Education*. London: Kogan Page.

Mouth (1994) 'ADAPT rolls over Washington', *Mouth*, V, 2, 10–12. New York: Free Hand Press Inc.

Myers, J. A. (1970) *Tuberculosis: A Half Century of Study and Conquest*. St Louis, MO: Warren H. Green Inc.

Olesker, S. (1992) 'Setting the agenda: student participation on a multi-media learning scheme' in Booth, T., Swann, W., Masterton, M. and Potts, P. (eds) *Curricula for Diversity in Education*. London: Routledge.

de Oliveira, W. Baizerman, M. and Pellet, L. (1992) 'Street children in Brazil and their helpers: comparative views on aspirations and the future', *International Social Work*, 35, 2, 163–76.

Oliver, M. (1992) 'Changing the social relations of research production?', *Disability, Handicap and Society*, 7, 2, 101–14.

Pearson, A. and Aloysius, C. (1994) *The Big Foot: Museums and Children with Learning Difficulties*. London: British Museum Press.

Peters, S. (1995) 'Disability baggage: changing the educational research terrain' in Clough, P. and Barton, L. (eds) *Making Difficulties*. London: Paul Chapman.

Phtiaka, H. (1997) *Special Kids for Special Treatment?* London: Falmer Press.

Pointon, A. and Davies, C. (1997) *Framed: Interrogating Disability in the Media*. London: British Film Institute.

Pratt, J. (1997) 'The polytechnic legacy: lessons from history' in Gokulsing, K. and Da Costa, C. (eds) *Usable Knowledge as the Goal of University Education*. Lampeter: Edwin Mellen Press.

Pritchard, D. (1963) *Education and the Handicapped, 1760–1960*. London: Routledge and Kegan Paul.

Ramcharan, P., Roberts, G., Grant, G. and Borland, J. (eds) (1977) *Empowerment in Everyday Life*. London: Jessica Kingsley.

Rothmans, S. (1994) *Living in the Shadow of Death: Tuberculosis and the Social Experience of Illness in American History*. New York: Basic Books.

Santiago-Irizarry, V. (1996) 'Culture as cure', *Cultural Anthropology*, 11, 1, 3–24.

Schirmacher, K. (1912) *The Modern Woman's Rights Movement*. New York: Macmillan.

Schwandt, T. (1996) 'Notes on being an interpretivist' in Heshasing, L. and Ballard, K. (eds) *From Positivism to Interpretivism and Beyond*. New York: Teachers College Press.

Schwartz, D. (1997) *Who Cares? Rediscovering Community*. Boulder, CO: Westview Press.

Sen, A. (1981) *Poverty and Famines: An Essay on Entitlement and Deprivation*. Oxford: Clarendon Press.

Shakespeare, T. (1997) 'Reviewing the past, developing the future', *The Skill Journal*, 58, 8–11.

SIAST (1995) *Teaching Students with Disabilities: A Guidebook for Faculty and Staff*. Saskatchewan Institute of Applied Science and Technology.

Simmons, K. (1996) 'In defence of entitlement', *Support for Learning*, 11, 105–8.

Slee, R. (1995) *Changing Theories and Practices of Discipline*. London: The Falmer Press.

Smith Livdahl, B., Smart, K., Wallman, J., Krinke, Herbert T., Kramer Geiger, D. and Anderson, J. (1995) *Stories from Response-Centered Classrooms*. New York: Teachers College Press.

Sounes, H. (1995) *Fred and Rose*. London: Warner Books.

Stone, E. (1996) 'A law to protect, a law to prevent: contextualising disability legislation in China', *Disability and Society*, 11, 4, 469–83.

Teller, M. (1988) *The Tuberculosis Movement: A Public Health Campaign in the Progressive Era*. New York: Greenwood Press.

Thomas, E. (1977) 'Researching values in cross-cultural contexts', paper in conference on 'Values and the Curriculum', Institute of Education, University of London, 10–11 April 1997.

Travis, A. (1996) 'Jailhouse Britain', *The Guardian*, 26 October 1996, 1.

Trevarthen, C., Aitken, K. Papoudi, D. and Robarts, J. (1996) *Children with Autism*. London: Jessica Kingsley.

Viewpoint (1997) 'Would you trust these men?' *Viewpoint* (Mencap Journal) 20, July, 3.

Walinski-Kiehl, R. (1988) ' "Godly states", confessional conflict and witch-hunting in early modern Germany', *Mentalities*, 5, 2, 13–24.

Walker, J. (1997) 'Unfortunate or scrounger? Ambivalence, stereotype and the adult unemployed', *International Journal of Inclusive Education*, 1, 2, 189–205.

Ward, L. (1997) *Seen and Heard*. York: Joseph Rowntree Foundation.

Wedell, K. (1993) 'Special needs education: the next 25 years' in National Commission on Education, *Briefings*. London: Heinemann.

Weiss, M (1997) 'Territorial isolation and physical deformity: Israeli parents' reaction to disabled children', *Disability and Society*, 12, 2, 259–71.

Welsh, I. (1996) *Ecstasy*. London: Jonathan Cape.

Wendell, S. (1996) *The Rejected Body: Feminist Philosophical Reflections on Disability*. London: Routledge.

Wodrich, D. (1994) *Attention Deficit Hyperactivity Disorder*. Baltimore: Paul H. Brookes Publishing Co.

Woodward, J. (1995) 'What is happening to CILs?', *The Disability Rag and Resource*, May/June, 21–4.

Wyse, T., Reid, F., Baker, C., Hawes, B., DeMorgan, A., Allen, A., Wittich, W., Porter, G., Mower, A. and Duppa, B. (1837) *Central Society of Education*. London: Taylor and Walton.

Yarnit, M. (1997) 'A telling tale of three cities', *Guardian Education*, 3 June 1997, 4.

Yuan, D. (1996) 'The celebrity freak: Michael Jackson's "Grotesque Glory"' in Garland Thomson, R. (ed.) *Freakery*. New York: New York University.

Index

Aloysius, C.   68–71, 75–6
art appreciation   68–71
attention deficit hyperactivity disorder (ADHD)   43–4
autism   42–3

Bar-On, A.   22–4, 32, 43, 54
Board Schools   11–13
Burt, C.   7, 9, 10

challenging behaviour   16–17, 21
child witches   18–19
choice and currency of labels   37, 45
colonialism   58
community   46–7
    caring communities   47–8
        educational   48–51
        international   52–4
    and collaboration   75–6
    values   54

developing world   30–3, 54–6
disability arts   73–5
disability culture   51–2
disability studies   62–3
dyslexia   38–40

emancipation   59
E-mapping   37, 44–5, 46
empowerment   61–2
    and popular culture   63–4
    values and limits   65

entitlement   41

family, isolation in   56–8

inclusive education   40

labelling and need   41
Ladle, J.   73–6

Mazurek, K.   40, 41
medical intervention   30
medical model   26–7
Miles, M.   31, 33
multimedia project   71–3

Olesker, S.   71–3, 75–6

reading   7–11, 13–14

Schirmacher, K.   59–60
Schwartz, D.   47, 51, 57, 67, 73
Sen, A.   37, 40, 45
social model of disability   29–30

tuberculosis   27–9

values   35, 40

Winzer, M.   40, 41
women's rights   59–60